HOW TO WRITE PSYCHOLOGY PAPERS

A Student's Survival Guide for Psychology
and Related Fields

Janina M. Jolley/ Clarion University of Pennsylvania
Peter A. Keller/ Mansfield University
J. Dennis Murray/ Mansfield University

PROFESSIONAL RESOURCE EXCHANGE, INC.
P. O. Box 15560/ Sarasota FL 34277-1560

107021

Professional Resource Exchange, Inc.
P. O. Box 15560/ Sarasota FL 34277-1560

Printed in the United States of America

ISBN 0-943158-08-7

Library of Congress Catalog Card Number: 84-60999

Acknowledgement: The American Psychological Association (APA) has granted
permission for this guide to summarize the style described in the *Publication
Manual of the American Psychological Association* (3rd edition, copyright 1983).
APA does not endorse this guide and is not responsible for errors or deviations from
Publication Manual style. This guide is not a substitute for the *Publication Manual*
which contains important information for authors submitting manuscripts to
journals.

PREFACE

The idea for *How to Write Psychology Papers* grew from our experience as psychology instructors who often found ourselves frustrated by undergraduate student papers that missed the mark. We've tried various strategies for helping students improve their papers—handouts, checklists, previewed drafts, and so on. Finally, there was no escaping the conclusion that a straightforward and concise guide to paper preparation would be most helpful.

Our primary goals were to make this guide accurate and easy to use. We have focused on the problems we most frequently encounter in our student papers. We have been selective in our coverage and included only the information students need to tackle an undergraduate psychology paper. We have made the assumption that students who use our guide will have received their basic preparation in sound composition elsewhere.

We've also made the assumption that students can only learn certain skills such as effective library use through "hands on" practice. While we've provided basic direction, we assume that actual experience with things such as indexes, abstracts, and card catalogs is necessary. We've made a conscious decision to avoid too much detail in areas that might discourage or confuse students.

We've used several strategies to make the guide readable. For example, we've avoided unnecessary jargon, used an informal writing style where appropriate, and added a touch of humor to retain attention through what might otherwise be dry discussions. Key terms are boldfaced for easy identification, and important information is summarized in tables.

It is important to emphasize that this guide is in no way a substitute for the American Psychological Association *Publication Manual*. While we have attempted to be consistent with the third edition of that manual, we have aimed our work at the unique needs of the undergraduate. The *Publication Manual* is a comprehensive resource which is a necessity for authors in psychology and related fields; we found it extremely helpful in the preparation of this guide and are grateful to those who put their efforts into its development.

We worked as a team on the guide and believe that we each contributed equally to the final product. Many times we challenged, rewrote, and again rewrote each other's work, leading, we hope, to a better book. While we assume final responsibility for *How to Write Psychology Papers*, many individuals have contributed directly and indirectly to the preparation of this guide. We would like to recognize their assistance.

Mark Mitchell made helpful suggestions during the planning and writing of the book. Rhonda Keller and Claire Foreman read early drafts of the manuscript and offered useful comments. The support of all three (who, in addition, happen to be our spouses) is gratefully acknowledged.

Fred Batt is a skilled reference librarian who made helpful comments on the chapter which deals with library use. Several of his suggestions were incorporated into the final manuscript. Marilyn Bodnar also called several important points to our attention in that chapter. Joann Bierenbaum went beyond the call of duty as a copy editor and suggested many valuable revisions to the manuscript. We are grateful for her diligence in this role. Debbie Worthington, Eileen Coan, and David Crist were helpful in catching errors in the manuscript and in various ways moving the book toward completion. We appreciate their assistance with the task. Last, and most certainly not least, we would like to acknowledge the support of numerous colleagues and students who reviewed prepublication drafts of the guide and provided valuable feedback.

We would also like your help and feedback. At the end of the book you will find a brief questionnaire for your use. If you have comments or suggestions, please return this questionnaire to the publisher who will forward your reactions to us. We want to incorporate your feedback in subsequent revisions of the guide.

Janina M. Jolley
Peter A. Keller
J. Dennis Murray

HOW TO WRITE PSYCHOLOGY PAPERS

CONTENTS

1

INTRODUCTION

Writing effective term papers and research reports is one of the most important challenges in college study. Students often seem to respond with fear when they learn their term paper in psychology, sociology, or a related behavioral science requires a style somewhat different from the one they've used before. If you're in that position, our book should be reassuring. The style used in these papers is straightforward. Once you've started to use this style, you may even discover it's easier than others and offers several advantages.

This guide is consistent with what has become known as APA (American Psychological Association) style. APA style grows out of efforts over the past 50 years to define a consistent way of writing for journals published by the American Psychological Association. Because of its simplicity and clearly defined expectations, APA style has also been accepted by publications in many related fields.

In addition, students in the behavioral sciences are often expected to follow APA style as they prepare papers. Sometimes this becomes a little confusing because the APA *Publication Manual* (APA, 1983), now in its third edition, mainly addresses preparation of reports for publication in research journals. In this guide we'll show you how to prepare effective papers and research reports which are consistent with APA style. However, we'll focus primarily on the issues students face when preparing papers and reports for class assignments.

By now you may be curious about the main differences between papers in psychology and other term papers. First, there is a different system of organization usually associated with psychology papers. In this guide we'll show you how to organize and develop your paper to conform to this system.

APA style also differs in the way references are cited. Instead of a bibliography, papers written in APA style have a reference list. All the sources you've cited in the body of a paper appear in this list at the end of the paper. References are cited in the text by author's name and date. There is generally no need for footnotes as they are used in other styles of paper preparation.

Another major difference is in formal construction of the paper. In contrast to literary pieces, papers in psychology are generally based on a scientific method of investigation. Whether it is a term paper or a research report, your paper should follow a logical progression as you investigate the topic. You'll usually be expected to examine your topic from a scientist's perspective. This doesn't mean that your style of writing should be inflexible, but a scientific approach does require that you be logical.

To accomplish our goal of helping you write an effective paper, we've organized this book into a logical sequence of chapters. The chapter which follows will serve as your introduction to the library. Perhaps one of the most important things you can do is learn to make effective use of your library's resources in the behavioral sciences. Not only can this make a difference in the quality of your papers, but efficient use of the library can save you a considerable amount of time.

Chapter 3 introduces the basics of writing clearly. A brief guide like this cannot discuss all there is to know about effective writing. Instead, we've chosen to focus on how you can avoid some mistakes students often make. In addition, we discuss some of the writing conventions used in psychology. For example, it's important to avoid sexist language. This chapter is a primer on these topics, and you could read it next if you're not ready to explore the library.

Chapters 4 and 5 discuss preparation of the two basic kinds of papers commonly assigned in psychology courses. The first is a straightforward term paper. We walk you through the steps of selecting and outlining your topic. The main differences from papers you've done for other courses will be in the way you organize the term paper and cite references.

Chapter 5, which covers research reports, introduces the very specific format that is almost universally accepted for presentation of research in the behavioral sciences. Each report is expected to have an abstract, an introduction, a method section which answers specific questions, a results section, and a discussion section. There are precise guidelines which will help you organize this type of report under the proper headings.

Chapter 6 addresses the technical aspects of writing a psychology paper. First, we discuss such considerations as headings, subheadings, numbers, and abbreviations. Next we illustrate the correct method of citing references. You must provide a reference for each piece of information or idea you obtain from some other source and use in your paper. You do this by noting the author's name and date in the body of the paper and placing more detailed information in a reference list at the end of the paper. The chapter provides many useful examples of APA style.

Chapter 7 offers an introduction to "our electronic future." In the past few years something called word processing has taken the academic and professional world by storm. Because we expect this technological development to have significant implications for preparation of student papers in the future, we introduce you to word processing in this chapter. There are also several potentially useful adjuncts to word processing which range from simple spelling checkers to more elaborate systems for organizing notes for papers. All are discussed in Chapter 7.

In the appendixes you'll find two sample papers. The first is a brief paper based on library research. The second is a humorous research report. Both have been prepared to illustrate basic issues in paper writing.

A brief checklist for writing psychology papers can be found inside the front cover. We suggest that you use this to insure your paper is in good order before handing it in. Inside the back cover is a key to professors' comments. If your professor uses this key, you may need to consult it to understand the comments and corrections on your graded paper.

This guide is simply written and should answer almost all basic questions a student is likely to encounter in preparation of a psychology paper or report. We hope you find the text useful. We would, however, like your feedback if there is something that you think is missing or could be improved. We've provided an evaluation form with our address for this purpose. Please feel free to contact us with your suggestions.

Reference

American Psychological Association. (1983). *Publication manual of the American Psychological Association* (3rd ed.). Washington, DC: Author.

2

BEFORE YOU WRITE: THE LIBRARY AND OTHER RESOURCES

In this chapter we'll suggest some resources you'll find useful in preparation of psychology papers. To prepare a good paper will require some hard work as well as skill in finding what you need. One thing professors find annoying is a student turning in a skimpy paper with the explanation that the library didn't have any information on the topic, especially if they know of resources that haven't been explored. The first two sections of this chapter outline strategies for finding information relevant to a paper topic and for collecting and sorting the material you find. Subsequent sections define and describe the various reference sources you will want to locate and use. Chapter 4 provides some useful guides to defining topics and preparing outlines. It should be reviewed before you begin a literature search on a specific question.

A Search Strategy

You need a systematic approach to finding the available resources. Selecting the most effective strategy will depend on the libraries to which you have access. A good place to start is with an inquiry to the reference librarian or other individuals available at the library desk. Ask if there is a guide to using the library. Find out where the reference section of the library is located, and inquire about the available reference sources and indexes to literature in the behavioral sciences. Because each library is different, it's important that you **ask for help** until you really learn your way around the one you must use. Once you understand the library, you're likely to find it much easier to use.

After talking with a librarian, you should be able to come up with a detailed search strategy that includes a sequential list of the places in the library where you can look for information on your paper topic. Depending on the topic and the resources in your library, you may want to start by examining selected behavioral science dictionaries or encyclopedias. These are different from standard encyclopedias or dictionaries because they have specialized content. On the other hand, if you feel confident that you have a good basic understanding of your topic from reading in a textbook, you might want to go directly to the card catalog or certain indexes which will guide you through recent literature. There's no one correct place to begin, but it's important to have a strategy. One possible strategy might look like this:

1. Review the topic in current behavioral science encyclopedias or dictionaries to define its limits and clarify associated terms.

2   Search the card catalog under appropriate subject headings to prepare a list of recent books which cover the topic.

3. Examine books on the library shelves, and check out those which are recent and seem to give the topic good coverage.

4. Collect relevant information (taking carefully referenced notes) from the books, identifying recent developments regarding the topic.

5. Note the journals available in the library which cover the topic, and review articles from the past year which may not yet be indexed.

6. Check the last 5 years of the *Social Sciences Index* and *Psychological Abstracts* for current articles on the topic. (Your instructor may suggest you examine more than the last 5 years, or check another index, depending on the topic.)

7. Read and take notes on the articles which are available in the library and seem most relevant.

8. If your library participates in an interlibrary loan program, use this service to order books and articles which look important but are not available to you.

Keep in mind that the above list is just one strategy for searching for information on a topic. For a very brief paper you may not need to do a thorough search of abstracts and indexes. By contrast, if you're working on a major paper or thesis, you may want to search volumes of indexes and abstracts of many years. You may also want to check with a reference librarian about the feasibility of using an on-line computerized search of relevant data bases. You'll have to tailor the search strategy to your needs. In the following sections of this chapter we explain more about how to collect and sort information and discuss some of the specific resources which should help you.

Collecting and Sorting Information

We've suggested a strategy for searching the literature on your topic, but how can you keep all of the material straight? That's an important question, and you'll need an organized system of note taking to avoid chaos.

When you begin your search in the card catalog or an index, you may want to keep notes on a tablet. Organize your page so that the notes are readable and entered in a consistent fashion. The top of your page might look like this.

Call No.	•	Author	•	Title	•	Journal
						(Issue & Page Nos.)

Use this page to keep your preliminary notes. Next, look for the references on the library shelves. Scan each journal article or book to make sure it's really what you're looking for. You may discover that the material isn't appropriate. Be selective in this process. Check the lists of references at the end of articles and chapters to see if they contain other relevant materials you haven't found yet. When you find a resource you want to use, **make a reference card before going further**. (There's nothing worse than putting together a final draft and discovering that the reference for an important source of information is incomplete.)

Reference Cards

For each article or book you read, prepare a reference card on a 3x5 or 4x6 index card. Enter the information just as it should appear in your paper's reference list. The format for a reference list is in Chapter 6. A sample card looks like this.

SAMPLE REFERENCE CARD

Brownmiller, S. (1975). Against our will: Men, women, and rape. New York: Simon and Schuster.

HV
6558
.B76

At a minimum, each card for a book should contain the following information:

1. author's full name with last name first
2. date of publication
3. complete title
4. place of publication
5. publisher
6. volume number, edition, and so on.

For a journal you would include the following information:

1. author's full name with last name first
2. volume number (and issue number if each issue begins with page 1)
3. complete title
4. journal name
5. year of publication
6. page numbers.

If there is other information about the publication that may be helpful to you later, record it in a separate place on the card for future reference. Keep the cards, arranged alphabetically by author, in a safe place, because you'll need them when you prepare the reference section at the end of your paper.

Note Cards

If you expect the structure of your paper and its direction to evolve as you review the literature, you may want to keep all notes for each book or article on its individual reference card. When you have developed a fairly comprehensive outline for your paper (see Chapter 4), your task will be made easier if you rewrite your reference notes on supplementary note cards, dividing the material from each source according to specific issues or segments of the paper. Alternatively, if you have a good grasp of the topic when you approach the literature, you can eliminate the rewrite of your notes by putting them immediately on note cards separate from the reference cards. In either case, use care when recording information on note cards as they will form the basis of your paper.

Each note card should contain, either at the top or bottom, the author's name and the date of the publication of the material so that you can relate the notes to the original source later. At the top you may also want to write a heading or subject phrase which identifies the material covered on the card. This will later help you arrange the cards in sequence for the paper.

Your job at this point is to enter the essential information from the materials you're reading on the reference or note cards. This is a process in which you must be selective, writing only material that is

directly relevant to your paper. For the most part you will paraphrase or rewrite in a summarized form, and in **your own words**,
the information you want to include.

SAMPLE NOTE CARD

Brownmiller, S. (1975) Historical Context

In her introduction to the topic
of rape, Brownmiller's theme is
that rape has probably existed
since prehistoric time, but the
major thinkers of our time
avoided any discussion of
its theoretical implications,
e.g. Freud, Marx, Adler.

It's certainly permissible to copy material word for word, but do
this selectively. Only copy material that (a) would have the author's
meaning distorted if you tried to paraphrase it, (b) is so important to
the focus of your paper that it may need to be quoted directly, or
(c) is a precise definition. If you copy a direct quote, be sure it's
copied accurately. Place quotation marks around it, and note the
numbers of the pages on which the quote originally appeared. This
way there will be no doubt about the source of the wording when
you prepare the final paper. Never enter a statement word for word
on the assumption that you'll change it later. In all probability what
may have been clear in your mind when you made the notes will be
fuzzy when you're ready to write the paper.

Material should be entered onto the note cards so that each card
covers a focused subject or idea related to the subject identified at
the top of the card. Since each note card will derive from only one
reference, it follows that the information from a single source may
require several note cards, one for each subject. Similarly, each subject may be represented by several note cards, one for each relevant
reference.

If you are fairly comfortable with your topic or experienced in writing papers, you will be able to develop an outline from your note cards and your prior knowledge. If you are inexperienced, you may find it necessary to finish your literature search, formulate an outline, and then rewrite your notes on individual note cards. In either event, these cards will prove invaluable, for they constitute the building blocks of the paper to follow. Once arranged in accordance with your outline, the notes will only need to be linked together to provide the substance of much of the paper. Now that you know how to organize information, we'll discuss some of the principle resources for your paper.

Dictionaries and Encyclopedias

Before looking in a card catalog or index, you may want to explore the behavioral science dictionaries and encyclopedias available in your library. They are usually grouped close to each other in a reference section. These volumes can sometimes be of help in focusing your topic or suggesting related areas to explore. They can also help define terms, which will enable you to do a more effective search in the card catalog or various indexes. Be careful to note the publication dates of these references because subject areas can change rapidly in the behavioral sciences. The older a volume, the less likely it is to be of use to you.

We've not suggested specific volumes here because there is considerable variation among libraries in holdings and a wide range of useful references in print. Your library may have a list of available dictionaries and indexes in the behavioral sciences. Ask for a copy in the reference section. Also, find out whether the staff of your library includes a specialist in the social or behavioral sciences—such an individual can be extremely helpful.

The *Thesaurus of Psychological Index Terms* can also be quite helpful when defining and clarifying terms. Its use in relation to the *Psychological Abstracts* is discussed later in this chapter.

Card Catalogs

One of the most valuable sources of information in preparation of your paper will be the card catalog. This contains cards arranged alphabetically by title, subject, and author, listing all of the books available in your library. Unless you already know that you're looking for a specific book or the works of a particular author, you'll want to begin with the subject part of the catalog.

Before you forge ahead, be sure you can read the information on the cards. Your library may have material which explains more about the particular system used there. A typical card contains a call number at the top that informs you of the location of the book on the shelves. Also listed at or near the top of the card would be the subject, title, or author. In addition to such information as the book's publisher and length, you'll find toward the bottom of the card, a brief list of other subject headings under which the book is cataloged. That's often a hint that you should search under the other subjects for related books.

SAMPLE SUBJECT CARD

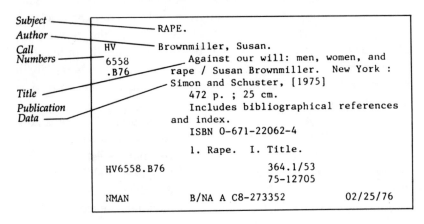

There are some important changes happening in the format of card catalogs. You shouldn't be surprised to find your library doesn't use the traditional cards. Some libraries have the material available in the form of a computer printout; in others you will use computer terminals to find the information you need. In either case instructions should be available.

Journals and Periodicals

Your library has a room or section which displays current periodicals on shelves. The order in which the journals are displayed will depend on the system your library uses. You may have the easiest access to periodicals in a library which groups the journals according to subject matter. If this isn't the case in your library, you'll be able to track down relevant periodicals by using the call numbers. Again, it's important to ask a librarian how the journals are organized and how many volumes or years are kept on the shelves before removal for binding or microfilming. Older journal issues may be bound together and placed elsewhere or copied on microfilm. Once you learn to use microfilm readers, you'll find that material stored this way is usually quite easy to find. In either case you should have access to what you want; you'll just have to look in the appropriate place.

Usually there is a guide which lists periodicals to which the library subscribes and indicates where to find various volumes. Journals are typically identified by their title, volume, issue number, and year. Generally each volume corresponds to a calendar year. Within a volume the issues are numbered. For example, **Volume 1, No. 3**, would indicate the third issue to appear in the first volume year. Sometimes pages are numbered sequentially across the issues in a given volume or year, and this can help you find the articles you need. Unfortunately, numbering systems vary from one periodical to another.

If you're not used to the library, don't be afraid to browse and identify relevant journals. Often you'll find there are several journals which specialize in the topic you've chosen, especially if the periodicals are conveniently grouped by subject area. It's sometimes useful to look through such journals to get a sense of the material available. Usually, the material in issues that have recently been placed on the shelves isn't yet listed in an index or abstract volume, and the only way you can find it is by searching journals on the shelves. Don't waste too much time this way; if your search in the appropriate journals is unproductive, it's time to move on to an index.

Finding Recent Information

A valuable source of recent information is a listing called *Current Contents: Social and Behavioral Sciences*. This is a booklet which contains title pages from over 1100 journals. While it doesn't provide detailed information, it's a good way to search recent journals for relevant articles. It's likely to be kept near the abstracts on your library shelves.

The American Psychological Association publishes a series of abstracts on related topics. There are four: *PsycSCAN: Clinical Psychology, PsycSCAN: LD/MR* (Learning Disabilities/Mental Retardation), *PsycSCAN: Developmental Psychology,* and *PsycSCAN: Applied Psychology.* Quarterly issues contain abstracts from relevant journals. The issues are published 6 months or more after the dates of the journals covered. They provide a useful way to keep abreast of recent articles in a specialized area, but they do not promote an efficient search of the literature because the abstracts are listed by journal and not specific subjects.

It's important to note that these indexes and abstracts of recent articles are relatively inefficient when compared to printed indexes or on-line data bases which are described below. Indeed, a comprehensive search for the most current material on any topic requires the skill of a detective. The extent of your search for recent articles will depend on the importance of your paper.

Psychology Indexes and Abstracts

One of the most efficient ways to search the literature for information on your paper topic is to use a comprehensive index or book of abstracts. The editors of an index specialize in cataloging articles in an orderly manner, so that you can look under a topic heading and find references for the material which has been published during a given time period. An index provides a listing of articles, and sometimes books, according to topic or author. It doesn't tell you about the contents of the material beyond the information contained in the title. An abstract includes the same type of information as well as a brief, nonevaluative summary of the contents. Therefore, abstracts can help you determine the relevance of an article or a book to your paper.

The following is a list of useful indexes and abstracts you should look for in your library. It is not comprehensive, and you should consult with your librarian or professor for other resources which may be available. Following the list is a discussion of specific search strategies to use with indexes.

Psychological Abstracts

This volume provides brief summaries of the world's literature in psychology and related disciplines. Over 950 journals, technical reports, monographs, and other scientific documents are indexed by author and subject. A Brief Subject Index appears with each monthly issue. More comprehensive indexes are issued every 6 months. It is a key resource for preparation of psychology papers, and its use is discussed in more detail in the following section.

Readers' Guide to Periodical Literature

This is an author and subject index to selected general periodicals commonly found in libraries. While it indexes journals such as *Science, Scientific American,* and *Psychology Today,* its coverage of the behavioral sciences is not comprehensive. It would be of help in locating articles which appeared in popular magazines not indexed or abstracted elsewhere.

Social Sciences Index

This volume is similar to the *Readers Guide to Periodical Literature* but focuses on the social sciences literature. It indexes the major psychology journals which would be included in the collections of most college or university libraries, and it's relatively easy to use. Consider this as a useful place to begin your search for an introductory level paper.

Social Science Citation Index

This volume provides author and subject indexing of about 1,400 journals in the social sciences from around the world. Topics from anthropology to political science, as well as psychology and psychiatry, are indexed. A unique feature of this index is that it allows you to look up recent citations of any older key article with which you may already be familiar. For most effective use of this index, you should carefully examine the introductory pages or ask the assistance of a reference librarian.

Sociological Abstracts

This volume provides brief summaries of journals from around the world in sociology and related disciplines. It is indexed by author, subject, and source.

Social Work Research and Abstracts

This is a journal which includes original research reports as well as abstracts of articles in social work and related fields. There are author and subject indexes.

Dissertation Abstracts International

This is a monthly series of abstracts of doctoral dissertations from more than 400 universities in the United States and Canada. It is published in two volumes, with part A devoted to the humanities and social sciences, and part B devoted to the sciences. While psychology is indexed in part B, material of interest may be found in either section. There is a keyword title as well as an author index. Selected abstracts from this series are indexed elsewhere (e.g., *Psychological Abstracts*). A limitation of this source is that dissertations are usually only available through interlibrary loan from the university of origin, or by the purchase of a photocopy from a microfilming service.

Child Development Abstracts

This volume includes abstracts from professional periodicals and book reviews related to growth and development of children. There are author and subject indexes.

Index Medicus

This National Library of Medicine volume includes monthly references to current articles from about 2,600 of the world's biomedical journals, including psychology periodicals. There are author and subject indexes.

Bibliographic Index

This is a general index by subject to bibliographies in the social sciences, sciences, and humanities. Included are bibliographies which have appeared in psychology periodicals.

Subject Guide to Books in Print

This is an annual publication listing all in-print and forthcoming, nonfiction titles from over 13,900 publishers. Books are arranged according to Library of Congress subject headings. There are also author and title listings which appear in separate volumes.

Using Indexes and Abstracts

Once you've found an index or abstract which seems appropriate for locating information on your topic, you need an effective search strategy. First, look in the introduction to the most recent yearly volume, and carefully read any information or instructions which may be offered. Next, explore the various indexes to the volume as well as the format of the contents until you feel comfortable with the organization. In short, don't dive in until you know where you're headed.

Usually the first step is to make sure you're searching under the correct term or terms. Your previous work in defining the topic will pay off. You can also clarify subject headings by looking at the *Thesaurus of Psychological Index Terms* published by the American Psychological Association. This thesaurus is based on the vocabulary used in psychology and related disciplines. It provides related, broader, and narrower terminology and can help your search by indicating which specific terms to use as you look through abstracts or indexes. *Psychological Abstracts* are indexed according to the terms contained in the *Thesaurus of Psychological Index Terms*. Instructions for use are included with this volume. If the *Thesaurus* is not available in your library, carefully scan the subject index section of the *Abstracts* to look for alternate or related terms.

Next, decide how many years back you want to search. Many indexes cover the literature over several decades, but you may only want to search the literature of the past 5 or 10 years unless you're undertaking a thesis or comprehensive review of some topic.

You'll usually rely on two types of indexes while searching the *Psychological Abstracts*. An expanded volume index becomes available every 6 months. A cumulative 12-month, expanded index was also prepared until recently. In addition to allowing you to search at least six issues at once, these indexes provide considerable subject detail and will help you avoid reading abstracts which are not relevant. When searching abstracts written since the publication of the last 6-month index, you'll use the Brief Subject Index which accompanies each monthly issue. For each subject listed, the index will provide entry numbers which correspond to abstracts included in the volume. Whether you're searching in the brief or expanded indexes, you'll need to record the entry numbers on a sheet of paper so that you can search for the particular abstracts.

When you read an abstract which seems particularly relevant to your topic, copy the author's name, article title, journal name, date, volume and issue numbers, and page numbers on your note tablet. When you actually find the article and determine that it is likely to be used in your paper, you can begin your reference and note cards. Alternately, you could begin your note card after reading the abstract if you feel confident the article is essential to your paper. Of course, you should locate and read the original source because the abstract will not provide complete information.

Many behavioral science librarians recommend the *Social Sciences Index* as a suitable place to begin searching for information on articles in psychology and related fields, especially if a paper is for an introductory level course. It may be of less use to you if your paper is on a more specialized topic.

The *Social Sciences Index* contains references listed alphabetically by subject and author names. It is published every 3 months, and the issues are then combined into a cumulative 12-month volume. Because it does not include abstracts, you'll need to judge the relevance of an article from the title and journal in which it appears. Searching is a simple matter of looking through the alphabetical subject listings and recording appropriate entries on your note tablet. This index can also be of assistance in locating the works of a specific author.

Computerized Data Bases

In recent years there have been rapid developments in computerized or on-line data bases. Indexes and abstracts are stored by the computer which makes efficient searches of the literature possible. Not everything is yet stored on computer, and the searches are available from a number of independent services, each indexing different periodicals. Libraries subscribe to different services and may limit use of computerized searches. An important advantage of on-line services is that they provide rapid access to information and can cross-reference two or more key terms at the same time. Searches can, however, be relatively expensive. A simple listing of articles from recent years may cost as much as $15 to $30, depending on the number of relevant articles included in the data base and the length of time spent on-line. Because costs may vary from one library to another, you should ask the individual in your library who supervises searches for an estimate. University libraries often assume a portion of the cost for a search.

A search can only be as effective as the user and the searcher who must define and manipulate the key words for a search. The computer can't read each article; it can only search titles and abstracts for key words you provide and then list the information it has stored.

Because of the cost, most libraries will limit the number of searches, and certain charges are likely to be passed on to the user. Therefore, you'll have to decide when a paper is important enough to invest in a computer search of the literature. Some of the cases in which a computerized search may be indicated are the following: (a) if the topic involves complex concepts or newly coined terms, (b) if you require a comprehensive and up-to-date search, or (c) if your topic is interdisciplinary and you wish to search several data bases. If you're doing a short term paper which addresses a single concept, a computer search would rarely be indicated.

Several examples of computerized data bases are listed below. Again the list is not intended to be complete but to give you examples of the services available. While addresses are provided to aid readers who do not have access to searches in their library, such information will not be necessary if your library subscribes to an on-line service. In all cases it's best to have the help of an experienced searcher to avoid unnecessary costs. Readers from related fields may discover other computerized data bases which are more specific to their interests. A check with your librarian should be useful for this purpose.

PsycINFO

This service indexes *Psychological Abstracts* and selections from *Dissertation Abstracts* from 1967 through the present. A search may be completed on a computer terminal or requested by mail, in which case the user must complete a comprehensive request form. The form asks for a description of your topic as well as lists of relevant words and phrases. Typical charges for a search are in the $40 to $60 range, depending on the amount of computer time required for the search. Student searches obtained through a university library are likely to cost considerably less. PsycAlert is a companion data base which includes more current material before it is added to PsycINFO. More information and forms necessary to initiate a search can be obtained from the User Services Department, American Psychological Association, 1200 17th Street, N.W., Washington, DC 20036.

ERIC

ERIC is the complete data base of educational materials collected by the federally funded Educational Resources Information Center. Data from 1966 to the present are included in two parts. The first, *Resources in Education*, includes the majority of significant education research reports. The second, *Current Index to Journals in Education*, indexes over 700 periodicals of interest to educators. Information on such subjects as counseling and testing can be located through this service. Many useful materials that are not available elsewhere can be located through ERIC. The Educational Resources Information Center can be reached at the National Institute of Education, Washington, DC 20208.

Social Scisearch

This is an international, multidisciplinary index to literature in the social and behavioral science. The data base corresponds to the *Social Science Citation Index* which is described above. Material from 1972 to the present is included. More information can be obtained from the Institute for Scientific Information, 325 Chestnut Street, Philadelphia, PA 19106.

Sociological Abstracts

This data base corresponds to the printed version of *Sociological Abstracts* described above. The index covers entries from 1963 to the present, and abstracts are included for articles back to 1973. Further information is available from Sociological Abstracts, Inc., P. O. Box 2206, San Diego, CA 92122.

Final Comments

In this chapter we've discussed effective use of the library and related resources for preparation of papers. We want to reemphasize that libraries may be different from one another. There's no substitute to getting to know your way around your own library. Take an orientation course to your library if one is offered. Also keep in mind that successful use of the library requires time and planning.

If your library doesn't have everything you need, don't despair. You may be able to use a resource such as interlibrary loan. Libraries which subscribe to such a service are able to use a computer terminal to identify nearby libraries which have copies of a journal article or book you may need. It may take a few days, or even weeks, to obtain such materials from another library, and there is sometimes a charge associated with interlibrary loans. If your library doesn't have this resource, consider a visit to a larger library located elsewhere.

Resources

American Psychological Association. (1982). *Thesaurus of psychological index terms* (3rd ed.). Washington, DC: Author.

Reed, J. G., & Baxter P. M. (1983). *Library use: A handbook for psychology.* Washington, DC: American Psychological Association. This is a comprehensive guide to library use and topic selection written specifically for psychologists and psychology students. It provides considerable detail on search techniques.

Weaver, D. B., Baird, J. L., Bell, W. E., & Westerman, T. B. (1982). *How to do a literature search in psychology.* Richardson, TX: Resource Press. This is a brief book which primarily describes a search strategy for *Psychological Abstracts.* Strategies for obtaining articles are also covered.

3

WRITING CLEARLY

While every paper must have appropriate content, the clear expression of ideas is equally important. This chapter addresses some basic issues in composition and grammer which are fundamental to effective writing. After discussing methods for organizing material, we will offer specific suggestions about suitable style for papers in psychology and related areas. This discussion covers the errors our students most commonly make, but it is not intended to be a comprehensive review of basic writing skills. Resources for more extensive treatment of these topics are included at the end of the chapter.

There are also several matters of style not discussed in this chapter which are important to consider in preparation of psychology papers. This includes the reporting of research results and statistical information which is covered in Chapter 5. Other important conventions in writing psychology papers, such as the use of headings, numbers, and references, are covered in Chapter 6.

Getting Organized

One key to effective writing is organization. Before you start writing a paper, you should know what you're going to say and how you're going to say it. In basic English composition you learned to make an outline to organize and develop your papers. When you write a psychology paper you should start with such an outline. This outline should be detailed and include all your major points and citations. Once you've developed the outline, your task is to support each point you have listed.

The Paper

There are three major sections of most papers: the introduction (*beginning*), body, and summary (*end*). This is true of both term papers and research reports. The introduction serves as the readers' transition into the paper and essentially tells readers what you're going to cover. You should identify your main theme and the major concepts you'll develop to support the theme. The most important function of the introduction is to state clearly the theme.

Following the introduction, the body of your paper will develop and support your theme. Present your ideas in a logical and organized manner. The detailed outline you made before writing the paper should facilitate this task. Chapters 4 and 5 provide detailed information on the specific formats used in term papers and research reports respectively.

The final section of your paper, the summary, provides your readers with a conclusion and transition out of the paper. You should remind readers of your initial thesis, summarize the major issues raised in the body, and state your conclusions.

The Paragraph

The basic unit of writing is the paragraph. Rarely can a sentence stand alone. When you introduce an idea, it should be developed. In some ways a paragraph is like a mini-paper in that it starts with a central concept, develops that concept, and summarizes it. A good paragraph has two characteristics. First, it's unified; each sentence within a paragraph contributes to the same basic concept. You'll usually state the concept in a topic sentence at the beginning of the paragraph. Second, the sentences in a paragraph should flow naturally. That is, the ideas presented in each sentence should clearly relate to those contained in the sentences before and following it.

Writing Tips

While organization and content are fundamental to successful paper preparation, clear, coherent communication requires the effective application of basic writing skills. In this section we provide a review of some aspects of style and usage that are, in our experience, particularly relevant to students in psychology. We conclude with a list of resources for more comprehensive instructions.

Use Transitional Devices

One key to making your paper flow is to use transitional words or devices. Transitional words are helpful in tying one sentence to another and connecting different ideas within the same paragraph or paper. Common kinds of transitional devices include **pronouns** (e.g., "*Lewin* was a father of social psychology. *He* also....''), **repeating words or phrases** (e.g., "*Werner* proposed the orthogenetic theory of development. Many current developmental theories have a foundation in *Werner's* work.''), and using **synonyms or closely related words** (e.g., "*Cats* are a favorite laboratory animal for the study of sleep. As we all know, *felines* like to sleep'').

Transitional words can be used in many other ways. You probably already use transitional devices to make comparisons, provide examples, or enumerate. Below are several transitional phrases and their functions.

Function	Transitional Words
Make comparisons	Similarly/ however/ in contrast/on the other hand/ but/ likewise/ yet/ nevertheless
Augment your point	In addition/ also/ too/ and/ furthermore
Enumerate	First/ second/ next/ finally/ last
Give examples	For example/ to illustrate
Reach conclusions	As a result/ as a consequence/ therefore/ thus
Summarize	In summary/ in short/ to summarize

The first sentence of each paragraph may contain a transitional expression relating it to the preceding paragraph. If the new paragraph continues the theme of the preceding paragraph, use a transition like "in addition," or "furthermore." If you intend to introduce a new concept or wish to contrast, use "on the other hand" or "in contrast." Use "in conclusion" or "to summarize" if you are summarizing or reaching a conclusion.

Avoid a Pseudoscientific Style

In writing a psychology paper, you may feel you should write "scientifically." In attempting to do so, you may make everything sound complicated and obscure. This is usually a mistake. While your aim is to be scientific, a good scientist communicates ideas as simply and as clearly as possible. Avoid using jargon, big words, and long sentences. Remember, before people can evaluate your ideas, they must be able to understand them. Professors and experienced readers will not be impressed by papers they do not understand. Whenever you begin explaining something in a complicated way, think about how you could make it simple and brief. A comparison of the following two sentences will illustrate this.

Too Complicated: The author's hypothesis was a convoluted derivative of the structuralist model of cognition, modified to adhere to the more differentiated schema for primate cognitive processing put forth by William Ranyon (1948).

Better: The author's hypothesis reconciled the structuralist and primate cognitive processing models (Ranyon, 1948).

Support Your Statements

A key to writing clearly is being specific. Avoid using broad generalizations unless you follow them with concrete examples. Document or validate your points with data when possible. If you state, "The intelligence scores of mothers and their children are strongly related," support this statement with research findings or theory. For example, "In a study of 2,500 17 year-olds, Hollister (1983) found the strongest predictor of IQ was the mother's IQ."

A related aspect of style fairly common in psychological writing is the tendency to hedge or to adopt an attitude of scientific skepticism. For example, psychologists may write, "the results suggest...," or "the subject appeared to be...," rather than speaking with certainty. This may be for good reason, and it is important to carefully consider the degree of certainty with which you make a statement. You should choose words carefully in this regard. However, when you feel certain about a conclusion and have supporting evidence, your statement should reflect appropriate confidence.

Choose the Proper Tense

Choosing the correct tense in which to write your psychology papers can be confusing. The first basic rule is to avoid the future tense. Most of your paper should be written in the past tense. This applies to research reports as well as term papers. The reason is that most of what you are describing has already been done. That is, the literature you cite has already been written, and the studies have already been conducted. As a general rule, discussions of prior research, descriptions of procedure, or statements of results, are in the past tense. For example:

Literature review: Mitchell's study **found** (not **finds**). . . .

Procedure: The subjects **were** (not **are**). . . .

Results: Mean scores **were** (not **are**). . . .

While most of your paper should be written in the past tense, certain statements may be in the present tense. A rule of thumb is to use the present tense in a scientific paper for statements which have continuing or general applicability. Therefore, definitions or statements from a well-defined theory should all be stated in the present tense. Often when you are writing a term paper you'll introduce your personal beliefs. These should be expressed in the present tense because they reflect your current stand on an issue. In describing the results of an experiment, whether in your own study or in an earlier one, the past tense refers to specific results applicable only to a sample (e.g., when you use descriptive statistics like means, frequencies, and percentages), and the present tense refers to general or timeless results applicable to a population as confirmed by statistical tests of significance. The following examples should help:

Definition: Drever **defines**. . . . In this experiment pain **is**. . . .

Theory: The orthogenetic theory **states** that. . . . Freud **says**. . . .

Hypothesis: Memory **was** not **expected** to correlate with motivation.

Results: Mitchell **demonstrated** (past tense when referring to a particular study) that person nodes **are used** (present tense when referring to general findings). . . .

References to tables or figures: Table 1 **shows**. . . .

Write in the Correct Person and Voice

When you choose which person to use, keep in mind "who" is performing the action. If you report the methods of a survey you conducted, write, "I administered the survey to...," not "The researcher administered the survey." Use the third person when you discuss the work of others: "Horrocks found that...."

In research reports, the active voice is used extensively, but not exclusively. It generally makes the report more readable. For example:

> **Awkward:** The instructions **were read** by me to the subjects.

> **Better:** I **read** the instructions to each subject.

Most term papers are written in the third person. Traditionally, the first person has not been used in writing college term papers. However, this rule is being challenged by many instructors, especially in classes where students are encouraged to express their thoughts and conclusions. Similarly, use of the active voice, instead of the passive voice, is becoming more common. Although, the "old school" advocates the use of the passive voice, many people today prefer the active voice. If you're unsure about which person and voice to use, ask your instructor.

Make Sure Subject and Verb Agree

The most common grammatical errors concern *subject-verb agreement*. Singular and plural forms of a verb are sometimes incorrectly matched with a subject noun or pronoun. Every sentence must have both a subject and a verb. The **subject** is that part of the sentence that performs. For example, "*Mark* is an industrial psychologist." In the case of a passive sentence, the subject receives the action of the verb (e.g., "The shot was given to *Smedley*"). The **verb** expresses action or a state of being. For example, "Mabel *ran* in the Boston Marathon," or "The rats *were psychotic.*" Below is a list of commonly used singular and plural pronouns and verbs, properly matched in both present and past tenses.

I (present/past)	We, They (present/past)	He, She (present/past)
am/was	are/were	is/was
have/had	have/had	has/had
administer/administered	administer/administered	administer/administered
analyze/analyzed	analyze/analyzed	analyze/analyzed
conclude/concluded	conclude/concluded	conclude/concluded
conduct/conducted	conduct/conducted	conduct/conducted
find/found	find/found	finds/found
hypothesize/ hypothesized	hypothesize/ hypothesized	hypothesizes/ hypothesized
observe/observed	observe/observed	observes/observed
survey/surveyed	survey/surveyed	surveys/surveyed
test/tested	test/tested	tests/tested

Use Correct Singular and Plural Forms

Many psychology students get confused about the singular and plural forms of certain scientific terms. The following list should be helpful.

Singular	Plural
criterion	criteria
phenomenon	phenomena
apparatus	apparatus or apparatuses
stimulus	stimuli
analysis	analyses
datum	data
appendix	appendixes or appendices

Avoid Sexist Language

You may have learned to write using the generic words he, him, his, man, and mankind to refer to people in general. In addition, you may have habits that either subtly or blatantly support sex role stereotypes. Until recently such sexist usage was not questioned. However, we encourage you to adopt a nonsexist alternative.

Since 1977, the American Psychological Association has encouraged writing styles that support egalitarian attitudes and assumptions about people and sex roles. Below are some tips on writing in an appropriate, nonsexist manner.

1. Don't use the words "girls" or "boys" unless you are speaking specifically about children; use "women" and "men" instead.

2. Substitute "person" for "man" and "people" for "men" unless you are talking specifically about males.

3. Use the plural when you are referring to a class of people. For example, "Students prefer their classes...," rather than "A student prefers his classes...." The use of plurals will help you avoid the generic male pronoun.

4. Don't designate gender unless it's relevant. For example, use "minister" rather than "woman minister."

5. Remember to use current job titles, instead of previous sexist ones. Examples of appropriate titles are: police officer, flight attendant, postal worker, secretary (not office girl).

Additional Resources

This chapter surveys basic issues of style that should be kept in mind in the construction of a psychology paper. However, the coverage is not comprehensive, and you may need a more thorough review of writing skills. The following references will be helpful if you want more information about effective composition.

American Psychological Association. (1983). *Publication manual of the American Psychological Association* (3rd ed.). Washington, DC: Author.

Copperud, R. H. (1980). *American usage and style: The consensus*. New York: Van Nostrand Reinhold.

Ross-Larson, B. (1982). *Edit yourself*. New York: Norton.

Strunk, W., Jr., & White, E. B. (1979). *The elements of style* (3rd ed.). New York: Macmillan.

4

PREPARING TERM PAPERS

In the course of your college career, you will often be expected to explore independently a single, focused topic related to some subject and produce a "term paper." This product of your independent study should show both you and your professor that you've really sunk your teeth into a topic. You should demonstrate a thorough understanding of the "state of the art" in the area and be able to write clearly about it. Your effort might involve proposing solutions to key problems, suggesting a research project that would further knowledge in the area, or organizing several subareas of interest into a larger model of understanding.

To help you prepare a term paper, this chapter will ask you to consider some basic questions and then suggest ways you can insure that your best efforts pay off. First, consider three questions that may be critical to getting started:

- **Do I understand what the professor really wants?**
- **What are reasonable goals for me to accomplish?**
- **How much motivation and enthusiasm do I have for this project?**

The first question is probably the most important one if you're to complete the technical requirements of the assignment successfully. Many professors provide written statements of paper requirements to their students. These vary in length and specificity; if you have a written statement of the assignment, read it very carefully (several times). Ask yourself if you understand what you are being asked to do, and what parts you could misinterpret. The parts that are ambiguous or confusing to you are the most important to clarify with your professor. If the assignment is given verbally in class, it is more important for you to ask directly for the information you need. Professors often feel that students pursue improper assumptions about the expectations for an assignment because they neglect to ask questions. Your responsibility to take charge of your education and understand an assignment is no less than the professor's responsibility to treat you fairly and inform you thoroughly of expectations.

Contrary to many student fantasies, professors do not give the term paper assignment to make your life miserable or merely to put you through a ritual exercise. They hope you will get excited by exploring a single topic in depth, moving beyond a superficial understanding and beginning to see complex issues at a deeper level. By preparing a paper, you have the opportunity to try on the role of a scholar and apply the methods of scientific inquiry to a real problem. If you clearly understand these expectations and your own attitudes in response, then you can do a lot to forestall later grading surprises and disappointment.

The second question, concerning goals, follows from your answers to the first and may be asked in several ways: Does the task require just a library research effort and subsequent regurgitation? Am I expected to do more? How much more? Do I just want to pass this requirement, or am I seriously interested in learning about a topic in greater depth? Can I allow myself to approach this task in the spirit of a scholar? When the paper is completed, do I want to feel that I went as far as I could with my learning in this area, or will I be satisfied with only a partial effort? Honest answers to these questions will clarify the actual term paper task.

Motivation is the third basic ingredient. Term papers are rarely the only major task of a semester or quarter, and you are constantly forced to ration and allocate your energies. Again, an honest analysis of your intentions will forestall unexpected outcomes. At least be aware that if you give less than enthusiastic attention to this paper, your professor can be expected to detect that fact in your final product and to grade you accordingly.

A problem related to motivation is procrastination. Most of the problems students encounter in doing term papers involve inadequate planning and the failure to allocate sufficient time to the task. A sure formula for disappointment is to put off until too late important tasks required by the project (such as ordering books through interlibrary loan).

Getting Down to Business

With these questions satisfactorily answered you will be ready to begin the term paper project. Completing the task will require these steps:

- **Choosing a topic**
- **Searching the literature**
- **Reading and organizing what you find**
- **Picking a concrete goal for the paper**
- **Outlining the paper**
- **Writing a first draft**
- **Editing and rewriting**

We will consider each of these in turn.

Choosing a Topic

If your professor has given you a list of suggested topics, you should, of course, take those suggestions seriously. Often, however, you are asked to choose a topic on your own. One way to do this is to step back from your day-to-day immersion in the course and take a broad view of the course content, the breadth of the topics covered, their meaning to you, and their application to your experience, or to "real world" situations that interest you. Examining your textbook from this perspective, skimming its table of contents, index, and chapter subheadings (especially those chapters you haven't yet read), can be very helpful, and should help you decide on a topic that will sustain your interest and enthusiasm. It's also helpful at this stage to look for a topic that, perhaps from class lectures or your text, you know generates controversy or interesting questions, or leaves you room to participate in problem solving.

Once you have some preliminary ideas, read what is readily available on the topic in your text or library. Talk to other students out of class or even in class, with your professor's permission. Your professor is a major resource and should be approached to help clarify your choice. However, don't expect your professor to welcome a visit which begins with, "I can't think of anything to write a paper on." Professors much prefer directing your thinking to doing it for you.

It's important to select a topic which is appropriate in terms of its level of difficulty. A topic which is too broad will lead to a superficial paper without an adequate focus. A topic which is too narrow will make it difficult for you to find enough relevant material, or what you discover may be too complex for you. What is appropriate will also depend upon the level of your course. A topic which might be suitable for an introductory course would be too broad for an advanced course. Some examples will illustrate the problem.

	Introductory Course	More Advanced Course
Too Broad:	Emotional Disturbances	Schizophrenia
Too Narrow:	Habit Disorders in Children	Speech Problems in Childhood Schizophrenia
Better:	Behavioral Models of Emotional Disturbance	Causal Factors in Schizophrenia

One test of the appropriateness of your topic will be the amount of relevant material you can find in the library. If you find too little, the topic may be too narrow; if you feel overwhelmed by the amount available, it may be too broad.

Searching the Literature

Establish early on the level of sophistication you expect to achieve with the topic you've chosen. If you're really interested in, or expected to achieve, a state of the art knowledge in the area, you'll need to start early and search the literature systematically. Frequently professors set criteria for the minimum number of books, journals, or popular magazines cited. Bear in mind that asking questions like: "How many references do I need?", or "How long should my paper be?", is comparable to asking, "How long is a piece of string?" Professors give answers only to insure adequate work and to avoid having many unnecessarily long papers. The amount of information available and its relevance to the goals of your paper will more appropriately determine the length of your reference list.

Refer to Chapter 2 for a discussion of how best to use your library and its extended literature searching capabilities. Start with a preliminary look at the subject catalog for book holdings in your area, and check recent issues of the indexes and abstracts most likely to cover your topic to see if there is at least some literature available. If you attend a small college or university, you will likely find that your library's current holdings need to be supplemented by interlibrary loans. This should cause you no major difficulty if you allow sufficient time for materials to be located and sent. You will need to be creative in searching for terms that are related to the one by which you know your topic. If you have questions about the search process, consider reading Chapter 2 again and consulting your reference librarian.

Reading and Organizing

As you read the literature concerning your topic, proceed by systematically taking notes; be sure to record what you feel is important. It is easy to get absorbed in the reading and to move on to other material without pausing to take notes. However, every good writer needs to accumulate notes carefully before attempting to write a paper. It is very helpful to write notes on index cards so they may be reordered at a later date in the sequence you'll be using them in the paper. Substantive notes summarizing a study or article can be written in the form they might be used in your paper. For instance, after reading a 10 page research report in a journal, your note could summarize the key points in a paragraph that begins:

> Throckmorton and Doe (1978) tested the effects of humor on reducing pre-exam anxiety by showing video tapes of early Candid Camera TV shows during breakfast in a large dining hall on the campus of a small midwestern liberal arts college. The subjects, 215 juniors and seniors, reported. . . .

By consistently taking the time to do this with material that has a high probability of being included in your paper, your literature review will largely be done when you sit down to write the paper. One word of caution is in order, however. Some detail oriented students get trapped by their note taking. They report finding it hard to screen their reading for importance or relevance and consequently write down everything they read. Some also find it hard to focus their reading and study in only one area; they end up with enough material for several papers instead of one. All of your reading and note taking needs to be guided by an ever evolving game-plan and goal for the paper.

Identifying a Concrete Goal for the Paper

By the time you've done more than a cursory review of the relevant literature in your topic area, you should be formulating one or more tentative directions or goals for your paper. Ultimately, you should try to decide on a single concrete goal for the paper. This should help you avoid many interesting, but irrelevant, excursions into related areas.

This concrete goal should be a statement of what you wish to have accomplished when the paper is completed. This could include: a basic understanding of an issue or topic; a proposal of a solution to a social problem; a research design that would, if implemented, help clarify an issue; or a set of guidelines to help practitioners deal appropriately with an issue in applied settings. It is crucial that you determine this goal before you've gone too far in your research and writing. Such a goal makes the actual paper writing simpler and more straightforward.

Outlining the Paper

With much of the literature review done and a goal fairly well defined, you're ready to outline the paper. The outline will make the writing much easier. All papers need a beginning, middle, and an end, but social science term papers typically follow a sequence like this:

Introduction

Literature Review

Discussion
(Your Contribution)
Summary and Conclusion

This list only contains the major areas. You'll need a more detailed outline for each section. We'll give an example of an actual outline later, but first we'll discuss the purpose of each of these major sections.

Introduction

This section includes a description of the social problem, research dilemma, or general issue you're addressing. A brief statement of the problem should put the topic in some historical, social, or academic context. You can also explain your reasons for studying the area.

Literature Review

This is where you report on the results of your library research and carefully articulate an understanding of what is already known in your topic area. The amount of material and complexity of information presented will depend on the topic and your goal. Always assume that your professor expects you to have done a thorough job. You're expected to write the following section (where you provide your contribution to the area) with an understanding that you're not the first person to investigate a social science problem and that you are "standing on the shoulders of giants," the scholars and researchers who have preceded you.

In the final paragraph of this section, you'll probably want to summarize what you learned in reviewing the literature and set the stage for the next section. This summary should highlight conclusions from past work that are generally believed to be true. In addition, it should identify discrepancies in the available data or indicate demonstrated needs that show a cause for additional investigation. In this way you will provide the link or transition to the material that follows, which presents your contribution or solution.

Before moving on from the literature review, ask yourself the following questions:

- Does the reader understand "the problem" and what is already known about it?

- Have I provided a clear rationale for proceeding to a "solution" to the problem?

- Have I set the stage for my contribution and provided a transitional link to the next section?

Your Contribution

In this section *you do something* with your learning from the literature, using the perspective you acquired from your professor and the course. If this section is to be a major part of your paper, it may have its own heading structure and organization. In many papers it would be titled "discussion."

Your contribution may take the form of a new analysis of the available information, or you may synthesize an understanding of several related areas that have not been simultaneously examined before. You might propose a research model or series of studies that could answer questions raised by the literature you reviewed. Alternately, you might propose a new treatment or social program which meets a need you've identified or a new set of guidelines for an already existing program. To do this effectively, it is important to maintain an attitude of modest confidence that you have achieved a thorough understanding of the area and that you have the abilities necessary to make a contribution.

It is here that you can demonstrate your own thinking and problem solving ability. This is not, however, a license to speculate irresponsibly. Your solution or contribution should be built on the existing literature and demonstrate the approach to data and problems emphasized in the course. For example, a student in a developmental psychology course might study the day care needs of working mothers' young children. Any analysis, conclusions, or proposed solutions would be expected to reflect both existing knowledge and a developmental perspective.

It is also important to maintain a distinction between your ideas and commentary and the ideas of others you've read. This distinction needs to be clear to both you and your reader. Always reference those whose ideas are similar to yours, providing appropriate support for your conclusions and eliminating any doubt regarding appropriate credit for ideas.

A Summary and Concluding Statement

Every paper needs a summary and conclusion. The length may vary, but you should attempt to describe where you've been in your academic travel through the topic. This final statement should show that you accomplished the task defined in your introduction and followed a logical path towards your stated goal.

A sample outline appears below. It is taken from a paper written for a community psychology course. An additional example of an outline is the heading structure of the sample term paper in Appendix A. Your specific outline may include many more headings and subheadings. Keep in mind the levels of subheadings you're using and refer to the discussion of headings in Chapter 6. Effective use of headings will help prevent run-on and poorly organized sections. A good outline with sufficient detail, organization, and logic to the headings gives you the sense that the paper will almost write itself. When you've prepared an outline that covers all the areas you feel are important in a logical sequence, you're ready to write.

SAMPLE TERM PAPER OUTLINE

PREVENTION OF ALCOHOLISM AMONG CHILDREN OF ALCOHOLICS

I. Introduction
   A. Statement of the Problem
      1. To treat or prevent?
      2. Barriers to identification and intervention
II. Literature Review
   A. Evidence for Risk
      1. Epidemiological studies
      2. Clinical evidence
   B. Previous Interventions
      1. Primary prevention
      2. Secondary prevention
III. A Prevention Plan
   A. Assessment and Identification
      1. Identifying high risk children
      2. Educating community gatekeepers

Writing A First Draft

If you've followed the steps outlined above, writing the first draft of your paper should be a combination of splicing together notes from your earlier literature search and filling in the blanks left in your detailed outline. Assume at the outset that you'll be doing more than one draft of the paper. Some students worry so much about every word they become paralyzed and unable to write. Allow yourself the luxury of putting words down on paper the first time without worrying about whether they are absolutely correct. Our advice to procrastinators and worriers is to write first, edit second, and save the worrying for the outcome of the next national election. You can always edit yesterday's awkward writing, but only if you wrote the first draft yesterday.

Just as in note taking, you may wish to write separate sections of the paper on separate pages which you can later discard, edit, or use as appropriate. It's helpful to double-space your early draft(s), whether you write by hand or type. This allows greater ease of editing when you may need space for corrections.

Editing and Rewriting

With a first draft on paper, the hard part is over. Now you can concentrate on refining what you said without the worry of what to say. You now want to edit for content, style, and organization. Have you said everything you wanted to say? Are all the sections consistent with the outline? Does some material need to be moved to another section, or should you revise the outline? Are you writing clearly (see Chapter 3)? Have you used a consistent style throughout and adhered to the proper guidelines for quotations, headings, referencing others' work, and so forth?

There are numerous approaches to editing. Some people mark on their first draft then rewrite. Others minimize rewrites by cutting and pasting (or taping) reusable sections into newly written material. And, as discussed in Chapter 7, editing drafts on the video screen of a word processor is clearly the way of the future. The important thing is that you not be afraid to experiment with what you've done.

The number of drafts necessary for a really "good" piece of writing depends on an individual's ability and experience, as well as his or her criteria for good. While students rarely allow sufficient time for many drafts, professional writers often do four or more drafts and then turn their work over to a copy editor for polishing. Like any highly refined technique, good writing is the result of practice. Your skill will look more practiced, the more you practice the skill.

When you've done one or more rewrites of your paper, consider these two suggestions before preparing a final typed version for your professor. First, let someone else, such as a good friend, read your paper for style, flow, and clarity. By now, you've become too close to your own words to catch any ambiguity or lack of clarity. When communicating to yourself, you make a lot more sense, being both speaker and listener, than when your words are read by someone else. Of course, your paper must remain only your work, but there's no reason why you can't make use of your friend's evaluation of your style.

The second suggestion is to read the paper aloud to yourself and listen to the sound and flow of your words. Take special note of places where you falter or have a hard time understanding the meaning of a sentence. These simple steps will save a lot of aggravation for your professor and eliminate distractions that keep him or her from attending to your main ideas.

Last Touches

A final draft, ready to be submitted to your professor, should be carefully typed with as few errors as possible. That means you must very carefully proofread your paper. Again, don't punish yourself by irritating a professor with little things: inaccurate spelling, typos, incorrect style, dirty typewriter keys, and so forth. Your ideas deserve the best showcase you can give them.

It's also helpful to inquire how your paper should be packaged when submitted. Not all professors appreciate the plastic binders you buy in the campus bookstore. Some prefer stapled or paper-clipped reports. Ask! You could save a few cents and please the professor.

5

PREPARING RESEARCH REPORTS

Writing a research report will require all of the skills necessary to prepare a term paper (Chapter 4) as well as the abilities to formulate a reasonable research question, design and conduct appropriate studies, and analyze and interpret data. This chapter presumes adequate knowledge in all these areas and is intended primarily to provide information about the special conventions applying to the construction of a research report.

There are six major sections in psychology research reports: the title, abstract, introduction, method, results, and discussion. In this chapter we describe the content of each section.

Title

The title is the readers' first exposure to your work. You should make it simple, direct, and informative. Avoid cute labels that might obscure the nature of your report. If there's some informative phrase you want to include, use a colon to add the phrase to the main title. Remember to "tell it like it is" so your professor will immediately know what your report is about. There is almost never a reason for a title to be over 15 words long.

Abstract

The abstract is a brief (one page or less) summary of your paper. Even though it comes right after the title page, you should usually write it last. As briefly as possible, describe what was done, to whom, and why.

A typical abstract has about six sentences. The first sentence describes the general problem area (e.g., "Pain has always been of concern to people"). The order of subsequent sentences may vary. Usually the second sentence refers to the number of subjects and how they were treated (e.g., "Half of the 60 subjects were given a mild shock, the other half were not"). A third sentence explains how the criterion variable was measured (e.g., "Subjects then rated their pain on a 10-point scale"). A fourth sentence describes the hypothesis (e.g., "It was hypothesized that the group receiving the shock would report more pain than the control group"). A fifth sentence summarizes the main results (e.g., "As predicted, subjects who were given a mild shock reported significantly more pain than the control group"). The final sentence, states the general conclusions of the study (e.g., "The results suggest that pain can be manipulated and are consistent with Jones' (1976) theory of pain").

Most researchers write the abstract after they've written the rest of the paper. We recommend that you write the abstract after you have finished the first draft of your paper. Then, use the abstract as an outline to structure the final version of your paper. If you use the abstract as a guide for revising your paper, you'll make sure that you've emphasized the important points.

Introduction

The introduction starts on the next page and does not need a heading. It defines the concept under study, gives a brief history of the problem (literature review), provides an explanation of why the problem is important, and offers a description of what you're going to do. In short, it tells the reader what you plan to do and why you plan to do it.

Defining the Concept and Establishing Its Importance

You first need to define your central concept (usually the one measured by the dependent or criterion variable) so that your readers will know exactly what it is that you're investigating. You may find a behavioral science dictionary or psychology text helpful in defining terms, but don't stop there. You want your readers to think about the concept in the same way you have operationalized it.

There are several techniques you can use to convince readers of the importance of your topic. You can start by giving a history of the concept. You could also emphasize that great minds (e.g., Aristotle, James, Socrates, Freud, etc.) have pondered the concept, that a number of people through the ages have tried to understand the behavior, or merely note the fundamental nature of the concept (e.g., "The first cave dweller must have wondered about. . . .").

Another approach is to document the importance of the behavior by presenting statistical evidence such as the percentage of people suffering from some problem or disorder. In the absence of statistics, you could use quotes from influential people or organizations (e.g., The President's Commission on Mental Health) to persuade the reader that your topic is important.

You could also present a real life situation that illustrates your concept. Giving an example of the concept is a good way to define it. If you use an example that is analogous to your study, your readers will be prepared for the strategies you use to define the variables.

Another alternative is to use a case study. Giving a vivid example of the concept is a powerful way of making your readers believe the behavior is important. Since graphic examples are so effective, they are commonly used by salespersons (e.g., "I ran into a fellow the other day whose house burned down, and he had no insurance. . . ."). If you skim through journals, you'll find that scientific writing effectively uses these techniques without sacrificing rigor or clear separation of conjecture and fact.

Review the Literature

If you've done a good job, your readers should become interested. They think your criterion variable is important and are wondering what's known about things that affect this behavior. Your next step is to tell them. Telling your readers about what's been done will satisfy their curiosity and make the problem seem more important. Citing other sources shows you understand the topic and that your study builds on previous work. Rather than try to cite every study ever done on your topic, select only key references. Include some of the older classic studies to provide perspective, as well as those done most recently which represent the state of the art and current knowledge.

Once you've selected key studies, briefly describe them. You need to demonstrate that you've read and thought about the relevant research. From your descriptions, readers should learn the essentials of the research and your reactions to these studies.

In short, your first task is to show that the general area of investigation is important. You should define the criterion variable and concept in a way that clearly relates to your measures. You should also demonstrate the importance of the concept and demonstrate that your particular study will clarify knowledge in this area by describing current and classic work in adequate detail.

Setting the Stage for Your Study

Finally, in the introduction you want to set the stage for your study. Your objective is to justify the selection of your predictor variables. We'll briefly define and list suggestions on how to justify five types of studies: the exploratory study, the direct replication, the systematic replication, the conceptual replication, and the theory testing experiment.

In the **exploratory study** you examine variables that haven't been studied before. You should:

1. Define your predictor variables.

2. Describe other predictor variables that have had an effect on the criterion variable.

3. Demonstrate similarities between the predictor variables you have chosen and the predictor variables used in previous studies.

4. Provide evidence that your predictor variables have been inadequately studied and are worthy of attention.

In a **direct replication**, you're replicating or copying a study without making any changes. You should:

1. Emphasize the importance of the original study.

2. Discuss reasons for redoing the study.

The **systematic replication** makes changes in the procedures or subject population of a previous study. You should:

1. Emphasize the importance of the original study.
2. Discuss reasons for redoing the study.
3. Provide a rationale for changes in procedure or subject selection.
4. State your expectations for differences in results, linking these predictions to changes you made.

In a **conceptual replication**, you examine a problem from a previous study but change the variables used to operationalize the concepts investigated. You should:

1. Emphasize the importance of the original study.
2. Present reasons for redoing the study.
3. Explain your decision to operationalize concepts differently and your preference for the variables you selected.

In a **theory testing study** you test competing theories against each other by comparing their relative accuracy in predicting or explaining the outcome of your study. You should:

1. Describe the competing theories.
2. Discuss shortcomings of previous tests of the theories.
3. State the relevance of the variables you examine to the theories in question.
4. Demonstrate clearly that the alternative predictions proposed for each theory follow logically from the theories themselves.

Stating Hypotheses

Having defined the problem area, convinced readers of its importance, and placed your study in historical context, you should make very clear what you expect to discover. Usually, the last section of the introduction includes your hypothesis or hypotheses. These should be stated directly and are usually written in the past tense, because they were formulated prior to collecting data or writing the report. For example: "I expected to find...," "My hypothesis was that...." (See Chapter 3 for a discussion of the use of active versus passive voice.)

Method

Having convinced your readers that the problem is important and introduced what you're going to do, the next step is to tell them how you tested these ideas. This "how" section is called the method section. It's usually composed of subjects, design, apparatus, and procedure subsections.

Subjects

Here you should describe the general characteristics of the subjects. State how many subjects you had (indicating how many males, females, blacks, whites, etc.), what ages they were, and how you got them to be in your study. You might also mention any other relevant characteristics they shared (all from rural areas, all geniuses, etc.). You should also indicate when and where they were tested, and whether they were tested individually or in groups. If they were tested in groups, you should state the size of the groups. If data from some subjects were excluded, you should indicate how many subjects were involved, in what research (experimental) conditions they were to be placed, and why they were dropped. You should also describe how subjects were assigned to the experimental conditions. The following example illustrates a subjects paragraph.

> The subjects were 50 male and 66 female, 18-21 year-old undergraduates who participated in the study to fulfill a course requirement during the 1983 Fall semester. Subjects were tested individually and randomly assigned to a condition. Data from four subjects were not analyzed because individuals did not follow instructions. Fifty-five subjects were in the experimental condition, and 61 were in the control condition.

Design

In this paragraph describe the predictor variables and the design of your study. If you're conducting an experiment, give the number of levels of each independent (predictor) variable, and indicate whether the variable is a between or within subjects variable. If your

study is a survey, describe other predictor or correlated variables
you measured (e.g., SES, age, geographical location, education).
You should then describe the criterion (dependent) variable or variables. Two examples follow:

> **Experiment:** The study utilized a 2 (male or female
> experimenter) by 2 (high or low stress level) between
> subjects design.   The dependent variable was a measure
> of perceived attraction to the experimenter.
>
> **Survey:** The study utilized a 2 (rural or urban) by 2 (young
> or old) between subjects design.   These predictor variables
> were correlated with measures of locus of control and future
> expectation for employment.

Apparatus

In the apparatus section, simply describe the equipment, stimulus
materials, and measures used. If you used equipment made by a
company, identify the brand name and make of the product. Even if
you didn't use any special equipment, provide enough information
for your readers to be able to acquire or reproduce the materials you
used. Give at least one example of a stimulus item so that readers
will have an understanding of what the subjects saw. You may wish
to attach a copy of your stimulus materials and measures in an appendix.

If you used a published test, provide the name of the test and a
reference. If you used a test or questionnaire that is not commonly
known (including instruments of your own construction), give a
brief description of what it measures, with sample items, and include a summary of information about its reliability and validity.
Also, include a complete copy of the instrument in an appendix.

Procedure

Here, you should describe the procedure from the subject's perspective, making it easy for readers to imagine themselves as subjects in the study. Excessive detail is not necessary if you include a
full script of the procedures in an appendix. You should be fairly

specific, however, about the differences in the instructions for experimental (treatment) and control conditions. Most researchers quote important parts of the instructions in the procedure section. You should include all the information necessary for a reader to replicate your study.

In addition to understanding what you did, readers should know why you did it. For example, in your study you might have a manipulation check. You would not merely state that "Subjects then rated their fear on a five-point scale." You would indicate this was a manipulation check to determine whether the subjects were affected by the manipulation in the way you had predicted. Any deception, single blind, or double blind manipulations should be explained. For example:

> Control subjects received a placebo so we could assume that any difference in the experimental and control group results were due to the treatment, not different subject expectations.

Debriefing. At the end of the procedure section you should tell your readers how you debriefed subjects. This should be a short summary, because in an appendix you will include a script of what you said to subjects during their debriefing.

Final Tips on the Method Section

Writing the method section will be much easier if you follow two simple suggestions:

1. The best time to write the method section is before or during the period you're conducting the study. It's best to write the section while all the details are fresh in your mind; later you may forget important details.

2. Preparing a method section is easier if you have written out exactly what should be done during the study. These instructions should be so clear that anyone could run a subject.

Multiple Studies

If you're presenting a series of studies or experiments in one paper, number them in the order they appear in the text (e.g., Experiment 1, Experiment 2). For each study include a method and results section. If you want to discuss each study individually, present a combined results and discussion subsection at the end of the method section for each study. Keep each "results and discussion" section brief. Once you've presented each study, you should have a major discussion section to link and synthesize the findings clearly. In the introduction you should have laid the ground work, so that your readers understand why each study was done and how they fit together.

Results

In the results section, the emphasis is on describing what happened, rather than explaining why it happened. Provide a summary of your data and your statistical analyses of them. First, make clear how you obtained scores. Often, you arrived at the scores in a straightforward manner. In this case, your first sentence might be, "Ratings on the happiness scale were collected for all subjects." On the other hand, some calculation or interpretation may have been necessary before you arrived at the score for each subject. For example, you might report that,

> The essays were read by three judges blind to the purpose of the study. Each judge gave the essay a score from 1 (poorly written) to 5 (very well written). The average of the three ratings was the essay's quality score.

Or you might write,

> Ratings on the six scales were summed to give a total happiness rating. This total was the score used in the analyses.

Reporting Results

Once your readers know how you obtained the scores used in the analyses, explain how you analyzed the data. For example, "The differences between the scores for the two groups were analyzed by *t* tests."

You can then present the important findings. The order in which you report results will depend on whether you used a manipulation check. If you used one, report the results of the manipulation check before discussing the criterion variable. In other words, you should describe the effect of the manipulation check on your independent (predictor) variable.

Next, report the results relating to your hypothesis. State whether or not the results support your hypothesis (e.g., "As predicted...," or "Contrary to the hypothesis...."), but don't try to explain the data. Save explanations and interpretations for the discussion section. Also report means and significance levels for significant effects that you didn't predict. Again, state that these effects were not predicted, but don't try to explain why they occurred.

Statistical Presentation

Your report of results will vary according to the statistic used. Generally, you should state the name of the statistic, the degrees of freedom, the numerical value of the statistic, and its probability. For example, if you performed an analysis of variance you might report:

> As expected, older adults were significantly more
> susceptible to learned helplessness than younger adults,
> $F(2,46) = 3.85$, $p < .05$.

The F indicates the statistic, the "(2,46)" are the degrees of freedom, "3.85" is the value of the statistic, and "$p < .05$" is its probability. If the statistic had been a t-test, you might have reported it as, "..., $t(16) = 1.75$, $p < 05$." For a Pearson r, the degrees of freedom are not usually included, so you report only the statistic, the value, and probability (e.g. "...$r = -.71$, $p < .001$."). Letters which indicate statistical terms should be underlined in your report.

Alternately, you may just report the statistic, means, and significance levels. Many researchers prefer this method because the inclusion of means will communicate more information about the shape of the distribution than degrees of freedom or values. Multiple means, percentages, statistics, etc., can also be efficiently displayed in tables you insert at appropriate locations in this section. These tables should be referred to frequently in the text, and always identified by number (e.g., "As Table 3 indicates...."). For example:

Ratings on the five point scale of fear (1 = low, 5 = high) were collected and analyzed using an analysis of variance. Table 4 shows that the mean fear rating was 1.1 in the low stress condition, while it was 4.7 in the high stress condition. This difference was significant at the .001 level.

Tables and Figures

Tables. A table is a systematic arrangement of data into rows and columns. Your most important data should be presented in table form. A well designed table can be both economical and informative. It should facilitate comprehension of your findings by illustrating relationships among variables that are not easily understood in text. A comparison of the following textual presentation and its tabular alternative should illustrate this point.

Learned helplessness correlated significantly with unity for all age groups combined (r = $-.71$, $p<.001$), with the correlation strongest for the middle-aged group (r = $-.91$, $p<.001$), followed by young adults (r = $-.81$, $p<.001$). The correlation was lowest for the older adults (r = $-.38$, $p<.05$). Learned helplessness also correlated significantly with centrality scores when all scores were combined (r = .46, $p<.01$). This correlation was strongest for the young adults (r = .73, $p<.001$) followed by the middle-aged group (r = .65, $p<.001$). The correlation was not significant for the older adult group (r = .19).

Table 1

Pearson Product Moment Correlations for Learned Helplessness

	Self-construct	
Group	Unity	Centrality
All age groups	− .71***	.46**
Young adults	− .81***	.73***
Middle-aged adults	− .91***	.65***
Older adults	− .38*	.19

*p < .05. **p < .01. ***p < .001

As you can appreciate from the above example, a table should include several elements: the table number, title, column headings, body, and footnotes. These are described below.

Table number. In the text, table numbers (e.g., Table 1, Table 2) are always expressed in arabic numerals. Tables are numbered in the order they appear. If your tables are placed in an appendix, label them with capital letters (e.g., Table A, Table B).

Title. Give a concise title to each of your tables, and underline the title to help it stand out. For example, Analysis of Variance between Gender and IQ Scores.

Column headings. There are several column headings with names like stubhead, column head, column spanner, and table spanner. Don't worry about memorizing all of these names: Your readers are interested in a clear and easily understood display of the data. Effective use of headings (as illustrated in Table 2) can facilitate such a display.

The left-hand column lists the major predictor variables. The stubhead describes the contents of that column. Table spanners are optional, but are often used to combine tables. In our example, data on vocal reactivity and nonvocal reactivity could have been presented in separate tables. Combining tables allows readers to compare two sets of data and is more economical in use of space.

Body. The body of your table is simply the numerical data; usually the numbers represent data compiled from each group (e.g., group

Table 2

Mean Reactivity Scores of Sheep With

and Without Tranquilizers

Group	Age in years[a]	
	1	2
	Vocal reactivity	
Black		
With	4.2	3.5
Without	9.4	6.0
White		
With	1.5	2.6
Without	10.2	9.8
	Nonvocal reactivity	
Black		
With	1.3	4.5
Without	9.1	6.4
White		
With	3.4	2.3
Without	7.2	8.6

[a]One year olds were 6-17 months, 2 year olds were 18-30 months.

means, percentages of subjects in the various groups obtaining specific ratings, correlations, etc.). Never change the unit of measurement within a column.

Footnotes. There are three basic functions of footnotes in a table. You may wish to qualify, explain, or give information pertaining to the entire table. To do so use a general note, indicated by the word "Note." For example:

Note. Numbers represent converted z scores on the general Student Anxiety Index.

If you want to refer to a specific column, group, or entry (a specific note), use lower case letters (e.g., a, b) as in Table 2 above. To indicate probability levels on tests of statistical significance, use probability level notes, signaled by asterisks as illustrated previously in Table 1. Generally, one asterisk corresponds to a probability level of < .05; two asterisks, < .01; and three asterisks, < .001.

Table Placement. We stated earlier that you'll want to insert tables at appropriate locations in text. Actually, you don't insert the table. Rather, you show your readers where you **would** insert the table. The table itself is placed on a separate sheet of paper at the end of the paper. For example:

Table 3 indicates that female hippopotami are more anxious ($\underline{M}$ = 4.67) than males ($\underline{M}$ = 2.1) in the Water Anxiety Test. However, the male hippopotami were. . . .

Insert Table 3 about here

Figures. A figure can be worth a thousand words—depending on how it is constructed. It's sometimes better to show a concept or statistical finding than to explain it in a lengthy discourse. All charts, graphs, and illustrations are called figures. They are highly informative but can be difficult to draw. If you have access to a computer with good graphics capabilities, many of your design and execution problems will be solved. The objective is to come up with a figure that is neat and effectively communicates information.

The most common figure is a graph. Although there are many different types of graphs, some common guidelines for their construction exist.

● **The predictor variable is plotted on the horizontal (x) axis.**

● **The criterion variable is plotted on the vertical (y) axis.**

● **The information presented on both axes should be clearly labeled.**

- The information on the vertical axis should progress from small to large.
- The unit of measurement should be consistent on each axis.
- The vertical axis should be about two-thirds the length of the horizontal axis.
- Data should be plotted accurately.

If the paper is being prepared for a journal, place the figure title and number on a separate sheet of paper immediately preceding the figure. If the report is for a class, your instructor may want you to put the title and number on the same page, as with the figure we've done here. Use arabic numerals, and number your figures chronologically as they appear in the text. As with tables, indicate where in the text the figure should be inserted:

Insert Figure 1 about here

As with a table, the figure should appear on a separate sheet of paper at the end of the report. The following examples illustrate two of the most common figures, line and bar graphs.

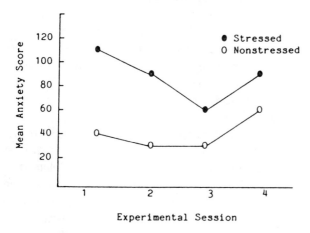

Figure 1. A brief description of the above figure goes here.

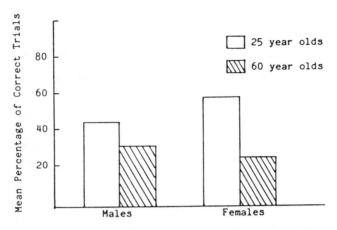

Figure 2. A brief description of the above figure goes here.

Discussion

In the discussion section, you should restate your hypotheses and the reasons behind them. Then, you should repeat and summarize what your data indicated about these hypotheses. Next, you can interpret your results. If your results are consistent with your hypotheses, you can simply emphasize the logic of your introduction.

Rarely, however, will your results fit so nicely with your initial hypotheses. There are usually some things you expected to find, but didn't, or some things you didn't expect to find, but did. If you obtained null results for your hypotheses, what went wrong? Did you use enough subjects, strong enough manipulations of the independent variables, sensitive and reliable dependent (criterion) variables? If not, how would you change the study next time? Sometimes you'll get ideas on how to improve the study from comments subjects made during debriefing. If you feel null results really represent the true state of the world, be cautious. Remember, the null hypothesis cannot be proven.

If your hypotheses were not supported, your next steps are the same as if your hypotheses were proven correct. You need to discuss your research in the context of the existing literature. Relate it to studies you reviewed in the introduction. In essence, comment on the effect your research has on current knowledge. If you wrote a good introduction, you shouldn't have difficulty documenting the impact of your results.

Next, you should comment on any unexpected findings. These comments can be speculative and imaginative. On the basis of these comments and the results relating to your hypotheses, discuss future research that might be done. Remember that no study is perfect or fully conclusive. Mention any weaknesses of your approach that could be improved by subsequent studies. Even if there are no obvious weaknesses, any study can be sensibly followed by others using different manipulations of the predictor variable or different measures of the criterion variables, or by studying different subject populations. Finally, you should discuss the potential of your results for "real life" applications.

Wrapping It Up

Now you're finished with the body of the report, but you still have to deal with references and material to be placed in appendixes. References include all the published material cited in your report. Your reference list should begin on a separate page following the discussion section. Refer to Chapter 6 in this book for the correct format.

Appendixes

If your report is prepared for a course, the appendixes might include the following:

A. The raw data—the subjects' original responses.

B. The verbatim instructions for all treatment and control conditions.

C. The stimulus materials or original instruments administered to subjects.

D. The debriefing—a statement read to subjects to explain the purposes of the study.

E. The scales subjects used to rate how much they enjoyed or valued the study.

F. Tables and figures in order of their appearance in the paper.

Appendixes are usually ordered according to their first mention in the text and labeled with capital letters (e.g., Appendix A, Appendix B, etc.).

You may also wish to check with your instructor to determine if there are some specific expectations for the appendixes of your research report.

Resources

American Psychological Association. (1983). *Publication manual of the American Psychological Association* (3rd ed.). Washington, DC: Author.

6

TECHNICAL CONSIDERATIONS

This chapter is concerned with technical aspects of the preparation of psychology papers. We will discuss conventions commonly accepted in psychology and many related fields. These issues are covered in more detail in the most recent *Publication Manual of the American Psychological Association* (APA, 1983). Our approach is generally consistent with this manual which dictates the style required for psychology journals. For a variety of practical reasons, this is also the style most professors prefer students use in preparing psychology papers.

Titles and Headings

As noted in Chapters 4 and 5 of this book, effective use of headings helps the writer to organize a paper effectively and the reader to understand better a paper's content. Therefore, we encourage you to make appropriate use of headings as a means of organizing your paper. You can see how headings and titles are used in the sample papers in Appendixes A and B.

First, your paper should have a title page. Unless your professor suggests a specific title page format, you should do the following. Center the title about midway down the sheet of paper on the first page. Under the title, center your name. Under your name, center the name of your college or university. In the lower right hand corner of the page, include the number and name of the course for which the paper is being prepared and the date it is submitted. While this style is slightly different from that required by journals which include a "running head" or abbreviated title at the bottom of the title page, it provides a neat, well organized introduction to your paper. In a manuscript submitted to a journal, the second page would contain an abstract or brief summary of your paper. This is usually not necessary for a term paper, but your professor is likely to require it for a research report.

The next page begins the body of your paper. Center your title in uppercase and lowercase letters about two inches below the top of the page. It should not be underlined. In the upper right hand corner of this and the following pages should be a page number. Make this page 1.

The APA *Publication Manual* allows for up to five levels of headings in an article. In our experience there is rarely a need for more than three levels of headings in student papers. The three levels of recommended headings are illustrated in the sample below:

Centered Uppercase and Lowercase Heading *(Level 1)*

Flush Left, Underlined, Uppercase and Lowercase *(Level 2)*

Indented, underlined, lowercase with a period. With *Level 3*

headings, the text begins on the same line as the heading.

Note that the centered heading is not underlined while the two which follow are. If a fourth level of heading is necessary for your paper, use a centered, underlined uppercase and lowercase heading as the second level.

Usually the material which follows the title on the second page is introductory. The purpose of such material is presumed by a reader, and no heading such as "Introduction" is required. The first time you use a heading will be for a section later in the body of the paper.

Items in a Series

Sometimes it is very helpful to organize material using a list. When this appears within a paragraph or sentence, items should be noted alphabetically: (a) **first item**, (b) **second item**, and so on.

Another type of list is made up of a series of conclusions or steps in some procedure which need to be entered on separate lines for emphasis. Each item is treated as a separate paragraph. These should be indented and listed as follows:

1. Item number one. The first line of each item should be indented. Additional material continues on subsequent lines.
2. Item number two.
3. Item number three and so forth.

Numbers in the Text

The use of numbers in psychology is somewhat different from other styles of writing. In psychology it is important to ensure precision and clarity with the statistics often included in a report or paper.

A rule of thumb for using numbers in your papers is all numbers 10 and above should be expressed in arabic figures, and all numbers below 10 should be expressed in words. There are, however, some important exceptions. For example, a sentence should never begin with an arabic number. The table which follows summarizes the use of numbers in the text.

Express as Numbers	Express as Words
Numbers 10 and above	Numbers less than 10
Ages and dates	Common fractions (e.g.,
Groups of numbers with some above and some below 10	two-thirds of the U.S. population....)
Percentages and percentiles	Numbers that begin a sentence
Precise measures or quantities	(e.g., Fifty-four percent of
Ratios	the group....)
Scores	Usual expressions,
Statistical functions	(e.g., Fourth of July)
Street numbers in addresses	
Sums of money	

Abbreviations

Abbreviations are used in a paper when they will help make a reader's task easier, but it's possible to overdo in this regard. Therefore, when in doubt we suggest that you avoid an abbreviation. Certain terms and titles have meaning to almost everyone familiar with the field. For example, MMPI can be used as a clear substitute for Minnesota Multiphasic Personality Inventory, and almost any reader would comprehend the use of IQ instead of Intelligence Quotient. In fact, these abbreviations make the task of reading simpler. As a general rule, you should only use abbreviations when they would actually facilitate the reading and be readily understood by all readers.

If there is a term which appears frequently in your paper and could be abbreviated, the abbreviation should be clarified the first time it is used. For example:

> Research at the National Institute of Mental Health (NIMH)
>
> has demonstrated this important observation (Johnson &
>
> Riggs, 1976).   The NIMH studies also found. . . .

There are also abbreviations which commonly appear in reference lists. Some of the more frequent ones are:

Vol.	for	volume
ed.	for	edition
Ed.	for	editor
p.	for	page
pp.	for	pages
rev. ed.	for	revised edition

The U.S. Postal Service abbreviations for states, for example, PA instead of Pennsylvania, are also appropriate. A period need not follow state abbreviations.

Citing References

One of the most important tasks in the preparation of papers in psychology and other behavioral sciences is the proper citation of **references**. This may seem a little confusing since most students and academic writers are used to thinking of **bibliographies**. There's no need to be intimidated by the change in terms because the basic approach is still the same. There are, however, some important differences, and once you understand them the preparation of papers may seem relatively simple. For example, since footnotes (except with tables and figures) are usually unnecessary in psychology papers, typing can be much easier. Also, terms such as **ibid.** or **op. cit.**, are unnecessary with the straightforward style of psychology papers.

References in the Text

When you discuss almost anything from another source, such as a book, journal article, or even a lecture, it must have a reference. Most professors will be very concerned about any information included in your paper which does not appear to come from your own thinking but is without a reference. Therefore, it's extremely important to reference the material in your paper which comes from other sources. If you are just starting to write this type of paper, it's better to be overly cautious and use too many references than too few.

For every statement that you have adapted from another source, there should be both a **name or names** and a **publication date** included in the body of the paper. There are a few basic ways in which a reference can be cited. First, the sentence containing the material can begin with the author and date:

> Jones (1983) was one of the first researchers to study
> carefully the annual spring migration of college students to
> southern beaches.

Second, the above style could be changed to the following:

> In 1983 Jones first began to study carefully the annual
> spring. . . .

Third, the author's name and the date of publication may be placed in parentheses at the conclusion of the statement:

> One recent study examined the annual spring migration of
> college students to southern beaches (Jones, 1983).

The reference may be linked with a single sentence or even a paragraph, but the material to which you are referring should be clear from the way you have entered the citation. If you refer to one article or book several times in the same paragraph, or on the same page, you need only use the date once, unless the reader would be confused by such things as other references with the same author which have different dates. The best rule to follow in this case is common sense. Always ask yourself, will the reader easily understand the source of the material referenced?

Multiple Authors. There may be instances when you use references with several authors, or several references which address the same material. Some of the ways in which this can be handled are illustrated below:

> Several early studies (Good & Johns, 1955; James & Stevens,
>
> 1962) collected data on student sleeping habits.

Note that an ampersand (&) is used between authors' names when they are enclosed in parentheses, and a semicolon separates different references. Note that the references are listed alphabetically and in order of publication. These would not be used unless the citation was within parentheses:

> Good and Johns (1955), followed by James and Stevens
>
> (1962), were the first to collect data on student sleeping
>
> habits.

Sometimes you will use a reference with more than two authors. The first time you cite such a reference in your paper, you should list all of the authors:

> Perhaps the most comprehensive study of "walkman"
>
> listening behavior was done by Johnson, Jones, and James
>
> (1982).

If you cite the same study again, you may omit the names of all but the first author and substitute "et al." for the other authors:

> One of the most interesting conclusions of the Johnson et al.
>
> (1982) study is. . . .

Secondary Sources. You may find it necessary to cite a reference from a secondary source. For example, you might find a pertinent article discussed in your textbook but discover the study is unavailable in your library. This is more likely to occur with older articles or articles in foreign journals. While you should be careful this doesn't occur too often in a paper, it's usually acceptable to use such a reference in the text. However, it should be followed by a notation in parentheses such as this: (cited in **author of secondary source, date of secondary source**). For example:

> Pavlov (cited in Hilgard & Bower, 1966) was the first to
> study. . . .

In the reference section at the end of the paper, only the secondary source is listed. In the text of the paper it is important to be clear about where you located the information.

Personal Communications. Sometimes you may learn about an important piece of information for your paper from a conversation, letter, or even a lecture. If you use this information in your paper, it should be noted in the text of the paper with the source's name and the date you obtained the information. For example:

> Several unpublished studies have also examined this
> problem (L. R. Goldbloom, personal communication,
> September 30, 1983).

Such information is not included in the reference list.

Quotations. You may wish to include quotations to emphasize important points in your paper. Brief quotations can be marked with quotation marks and included as a normal part of the text. Quotations longer than one sentence or 40 words should be set in an indented block without quotation marks, as illustrated below. Whenever you use a quotation, it should be referenced in the same way as other material, with the important addition of the **page number(s)** on which it originally appeared.

Brief Quotation:

> An important issue is raised by Walker (1978) who indicates
> "the unusual habit of compulsive and repetitive running

back and forth in a confined space while attempting to force a large ball through a metal hoop high above the ground" (p. 362) requires more careful study by behavioral scientists.

Longer Quotation:

Miller (1973) has also studied these unusual behaviors and draws the following conclusion:

> It is clear that the individuals who engage in this activity are often above average in height and lanky in physical build. This common characteristic adds credibility to the hypothesis that the compulsion to engage in such behavior is biologically based. (p. 18)

In looking at these samples, note that the page number follows the quotation marks, or, in the case of the longer block quote, follows the period at the end of the quote. It would also have been possible to arrange the material so that the author's name, the date of the reference and the page number followed the quote in parentheses.

> One author dismissed the conjecture about basketball as "a case of behavioral scientists failing to see 'the forest through the trees' " (Doe, 1982, p. 343).

Reference Lists

At the conclusion of your paper should be a list of all the references cited in the text. Only references which have actually been used in preparation of the paper should be included here. You should be sure that there is consistency between the citations in the text and the reference list.

References are listed in a very precise way, and it is important that you follow the format carefully. The first step is to be sure the material you collected on each reference when preparing the paper was correct—if you were careless at that point, you're likely to be in serious trouble here. Accurate spelling is especially important for the reference list.

The style we are describing below is generally consistent with the APA (1983) style. There is, however, one exception in that we do not include a separate section for reference notes. Reference notes constitute a separate listing of hard to find materials, such as lectures, personal discussions, and articles which have been written but not yet published. These notes are listed in the text by number, for example (Miller, Note 2), instead of date, and appear on a separate page titled "Reference Notes" just before the page titled "References" at the end of the paper. In contrast to references which are listed alphabetically, reference notes are listed by number based on the order of their appearance in the paper. In our opinion, this separate type of listing is unnecessary, if not confusing, for most papers unless they are intended for publication.

Reference Formats. There are a few reference formats which you must follow. They will be outlined here and illustrated below. One of the most common references is a **journal article.** It should be listed in the following format:

Authors' last names, initials. (Year of publication). Title. Journal Name, Volume number, Page numbers.

Murray, R., & Jones, J.   (1982).   Mating behavior of squirrels on the capitol mall.   Journal of Squirrel Psychology, 2, 123-128.

Another common reference is the **book.** It should be listed in the following format:

Authors' last names, initials. (Year of publication). Title (Edition or Volume number). City where publisher is located (including state abbreviation if not a major city): Publisher's name.

Jackson, J. K., Jackson, K.J., & Jackson, J. J. (1952). The effects of birth order on career selection (2nd ed.).   Green Bay, WI: Green Bay Press.

Order of Listing. References should be listed alphabetically by author, or in order of publication if there are several items by the same author. If the same author has more than one publication in the same year, they should be arranged alphabetically by title with lowercase letters placed in parentheses at the end of the reference (e.g., a, b, etc.). Where there is more than one author, all single author references by an author come first. Then the listing proceeds alphabetically by second author, then third author, etc. For example, consider the following order:

Albert, A. B.   (1982). . . .

Albert, A. B.   (1983a). . . .

Albert, A. B.   (1983b). . . .

Albert, A. B., & Allen, B. C.   (1980). . . .

Albert, A. B., & Brown, C. D.   (1979). . . .

Albert, A. B., & Brown, C. D.   (1980). . . .

Sample References

A sample list of references follows. The list is not intended to be complete but should include the kinds of references most commonly used in student papers.

Book Edited by an Organization

American Psychological Association. (1983). Publication manual
  of the American Psychological Association (3rd ed.).
  Washington, DC: Author.

Magazine Article

Bindrim, P. (1980, July). Group therapy: Protecting
  privacy. Psychology Today, pp. 24, 27-28.

Book With Two Authors

Goldfried, M. R., & Davison, G. C. (1980). Clinical behavior
  therapy. New York: Holt, Rinehart and Winston.

Article With Multiple Authors in Journal Paginated by Volume

Hartman, D. P., Roper, B. L., & Bradford, D. C. (1979). Some
  relationships between behavioral and traditional
  assessment. Journal of Behavioral Assessment, 1, 3-21.

Edited Volume in a Series

Keller, P. A., & Ritt, L. G. (Eds.). (1982). Innovations in clinical
  practice: A source book (Vol. 1). Sarasota, FL: Professional
  Resource Exchange.

Government Publication

Kopolow, L. E., Brands, A. B., Burton, J. L., & Ochberg, F. M.
    (1975). Litigation and mental health services (National
    Institute of Mental Health, DHEW Publication No. ADM
    76-261). Washington, DC: U.S. Government Printing
    Office.

Unpublished Manuscript

Murray, J. D. (1982). Training psychologists for rural
    roles. Unpublished manuscript, Mansfield University,
    Mansfield, PA.

News Article Without Author

NSF commission looks at science education. (1983, May). APA
    Monitor, p. 34.

Article in Journal Paginated by Issue

Sherrod, D. (1983). Consultants in the courtroom: How
    psychologists and trial attorneys are working
    together. Consultation, 2(2), 13-18.

Article in an Edited Volume

Zusman, J. (1975). Recognition and management of psychiatric
    emergencies. In H. L. P. Resnik & H. L. Ruben (Eds.),
    Emergency psychiatric care (pp. 35-59). Bowie, MD:
    Charles Press.

Typing Papers

When you type a paper the goal should be to make it as readable
as possible. There are several ways to obtain a readable paper. First,
all typing should be **double-spaced.** This includes quotations,
spaces between headings and text, and the reference section. The
first line of each reference begins at the left-hand margin of the paper. The following lines are indented five spaces, making it easy for
the reader to quickly locate a reference by the author's name.

Typing should be on a good quality bond paper, never on a translucent sheet. All margins should be between 1 and 1 1/2 inches. The typeface you use should be clean and readable. If you're using a personal computer or word processor with a printer set for twelve pitch, your right margin should be at about 70 characters. If your word processor is using a typical dot matrix printer set for 10 pitch, your right margin should be at about 62 characters. Please note that if you are preparing a manuscript for submission to a journal, margins should be even wider. Because a ragged right margin is actually more readable, you should avoid a right justification mode. Also, avoid hyphenation of words at the end of a line. Make sure dot matrix output is clearly readable by using an enhanced print mode if possible. Never use a compressed mode for printing a paper. On all pages after the title page, a page number should appear on the upper right corner where the top and right margins meet. After typing the paper, make sure you keep an extra copy for yourself in case the original is lost.

Final Comments

If this is your first experience with the style commonly used in psychology papers, you can expect to be a little perplexed. However, our experience suggests that the approach outlined in this chapter actually simplifies the process of preparing a readable paper. After you've attempted your first paper using this style, you should quickly become comfortable with it. If you have questions about technical aspects not addressed here, check with the current APA *Publication Manual* or your professor. The APA *Publication Manual* should answer virtually any technical question you may have about preparation of psychology papers and is usually available in libraries.

Resource

American Psychological Association. (1983). *Publication manual of the American Psychological Association* (3rd ed.). Washington, DC: Author.

7

OUR ELECTRONIC FUTURE

As we prepare this text there are exciting and dramatic developments in the field of microcomputers which have important implications for the preparation of student papers. The developments in hardware include economical and portable personal computers with capacities that required room size computers not many years ago. There is reason to believe that in the next few years almost all college students will have some type of experience with these computers.

Almost as fast as the more advanced hardware technology develops, exciting new software or programs are also developed. Much of the software is aimed at students, scholars, and other writers. It includes word processing, spelling, grammatical, and organizational aides. As a consequence, the task of writing should be made immeasurably easier as well as more fun in coming years.

In this chapter we briefly describe word processing and related software developments. Our goal is not to teach these skills but to alert interested readers to the utility of such techniques.

Word Processing

Word processing as it applies to most writers refers to a computer system which allows one to type and edit almost any written document on a television-type monitor (CRT), save the document for corrections or later modifications, and have it reproduced by a printer.

This approach has a number of distinct advantages over the traditional methods of dictating or writing rough drafts and then typing final copy. First, word processing allows you to examine what you've written on the CRT and make as many adjustments as necessary before you arrive at a satisfactory draft. This means that the necessity for multiple printed drafts of important documents is virtually eliminated after one becomes used to working on the screen.

Second, after a document is completed it can be handled in any number of ways. It can be stored, usually on a small "floppy disk" (similar in appearance to a thin 45 rpm record in an envelope), for future retrieval or modification. Or it can be printed, using a variety of printers, as a "hard copy." This is what would happen to most papers or reports. Alternately, it may be a report or paper on which you wish others to comment. If they have suggestions you want to include in the original document, you simply insert the disk containing the material, and revise it on the CRT before printing a final copy. Third, with appropriate equipment, you may be able to use your computer to transmit the document to someone else's computer via telephone lines. With the necessary device (modem), your microcomputer/word processor has the capacity to open up a new world of communication through various information services which facilitate communication among subscribers with similar interests. In addition, these services provide access to a variety of information, ranging from current stock quotations to a customized search of the psychological literature.

The available systems are of two basic types. The first type is known as the dedicated word processor. This system is designed primarily for word processing and may seem limited for the user who would like to adapt it to other functions such as statistical analyses, games, or program writing. Dedicated word processors also frequently have a high price tag, especially when their limitations are considered. The other type of system used for word processing is essentially a micro- or minicomputer with software packages which enable the computer to accomplish the desired functions. The advantage of such a system is that software can be purchased for a wide range of functions, or the user can write programs for specific needs. In short, the computer is generally far more versatile than the dedicated word processor.

Creating and Editing Documents

Virtually any kind of document or report you would want to prepare can be entered on the typewriter-like keyboard. As letters are entered, they appear on the CRT at a position marked by the **cursor**, a line or square which moves across the screen to mark the position at which you're working. In essence, you are creating a page on the screen. CRTs vary in size and are defined in terms of the number of lines and columns they contain. Typical screens for small business computers contain 24 lines. Widths generally vary from 40 to more than 80 columns, with the wider screen being more desirable because typed pages are typically about 70 characters wide.

Basic typing skills are important for efficient entry of information into the word processing system and make it easy to adapt to the new approach with relatively little training. However, even if you are a relatively poor typist, you may find some distinct advantages to word processing. If you make an error, corrections on the screen are easy since the text is not committed to paper until you've instructed the computer to print. As you work, the page on the screen scrolls to make more space at the bottom of the screen. Letters are entered on the screen at the position of the cursor. There's usually no need to worry about carriage returns—most word processing software contains a function called "word wrap" which places a word on the next line when the margin you have defined is reached. If you omit something and would like to insert a few words or even a sentence to clarify an important point in a paper, it's no problem for most word processing programs. They will allow you to insert or delete portions of text by giving a few simple commands. Before using a word processor to prepare a paper, review the recommendations of Chapter 6 (under Typing Papers) regarding formatting and choice of print.

We've outlined just a small sample of common word processing features. Most software allows the user to center headings automatically or to underline or print portions of text in boldface. If you would like your reports and papers to appear dressy, some programs allow you to have the text printed with both margins justified as in a book. Many programs will automatically print page numbers or page headings as you instruct. Some will search your document to find a key phrase or word. This is especially handy if you discover you accidentally misspelled a word or name and would like to check other occurrences of it in a lengthy report. Many word processing programs allow you to quickly insert key portions of text which you have stored elsewhere on your disk. For example, if you have a closing to a letter, a name and address, or a title page you like to include on all papers or reports, it can be stored on the disk and called into place with a few key strokes. Features like this can be real time savers if you use the same material frequently.

A word of warning—not all word processing software is the same. Prices for a package designed to run on a microcomputer can range from less than $100 to more than $500. Obviously there will be some substantial variations in software at different price ranges, and professional use will probably require software toward the upper end of the price range. Before purchasing a word processing program, we suggest that you carefully explore its features in relation to your needs.

Spelling Checkers

An especially interesting feature of word processing for students is the development of software which checks spelling. Usually these operate in a straightforward manner. Simply load the program and tell it the name of the file to check. The program will quickly compare the spellings of words in the paper with its own dictionary. Most let you add your own technical words to the dictionary so that you can quickly develop a list of frequently used words on the program disk. Even the most basic spelling programs will give a count of words in your paper which can be useful if you have an assigned length or just want to count the words in an abstract. In short, we're entering an era in which there will be no excuses for a misspelled word in a paper.

Other Word Processing Aides

In addition to spelling checkers, there are several other useful types of software which will be mentioned briefly. The first is a program which checks basic grammar. It will rapidly offer counts of sentence length and inform the writer of improper use of certain phrases. It's easy to use, but in our opinion the information it provides is limited. We expect to see more sophisticated versions of this type of program in the future.

Programs have also been developed to position footnotes in the body of a paper. This is an interesting idea, but there should be limited use for psychology students since most of their papers will require a minimum of footnoting. Other programs help to arrange indexes and tables of contents. Again, these won't be of much aid unless you're writing very long papers. A more useful program is designed to help organize bibliographies—in our case references. This program could be very useful in organizing a reference section as you write a paper.

Perhaps most interesting of all are a new group of programs designed to organize preliminary notes. Some use a card format similar to the one discussed earlier in this book. Others use a page format. All of them allow the user to search notes for key words and call up the related information. This feature could be beneficial in preparing longer papers, theses, or dissertations. It may also be of help to the serious student who wants to develop a computerized resource file for intensive study of a field.

We're confident that this type of software just represents the beginning of many similar and more sophisticated programs to come. As new developments occur, we'll discuss them in future editions of this text.

Printers

An important component of any word processing system is the printer. The quality of your print will determine the applications with which you feel comfortable in word processing. Many people initially attempt to keep costs down by choosing a relatively inexpensive dot matrix printer. While the prices of such printers (starting at about $300) and their relatively high printing speeds make them attractive, there are also many limitations. The primary drawback is print quality. Small dots are used to form the characters and tend to give the copy a "computerized" look. Although the dot matrix quality is improved in several new printers on the market, the results typically do not equal the quality of modern typewriters. Some users of word processing systems feel that dot matrix printers provide an excellent means of obtaining a fast rough draft of their work, but not a satisfactory final draft.

Many personal computer users can now afford so-called "daisy wheel" printers. While considerably more expensive and also slower than the dot matrix printers, the typical daisy wheel printer provides outstanding quality. A metal or plastic wheel with spokes that have characters at the ends spins rapidly and is hit by a small hammer to enter the character on the paper. An advantage of this type of printer is that the wheel can be changed to permit a variety of type styles. Even the slower daisy wheel printers, at about 15 characters per second, are faster than most office typewriters. The slower printers of this type may be purchased for well under $1000, while the more sophisticated ones may cost in excess of $2000. If you decide to purchase one, it will be important to learn first if it has all of the features you desire. Again, there are some important distinctions associated with the price differentials.

Other Considerations

Technical developments in computers, printers, and sophisticated word processing software seem to occur on a weekly, if not daily basis. We suggest that you consult computer dealers, current users, the books listed below, or recent periodicals devoted to computer use before purchasing any word processing system. Computer assisted writing promises to make your task technically easier, as well as more fun. In addition, it will improve the quality and appearance of your finished papers and free you to concentrate more on the content and substance of your scholarly efforts.

Resources

McWilliams, P. A. (1982). *The word processing book*. Los Angeles: Prelude Press. This is perhaps the most widely available book which discusses the "wonders" of word processing. Various systems and types of software are discussed.

Poynter, D. F. (1982). *Word processors and information processing*. Santa Barbara, CA: Para Publishing. This paperback provides a useful and nontechnical introduction to word processing and hardware. It is available from the publisher at P. O. Box 4232-0, Santa Barbara, CA 93103-0232.

APPENDIX A

SAMPLE TERM PAPER

Issues in Crisis Intervention

John Q. Writer

Upper State College

Psy 353, Introduction to Psychopathology

November 15, 1984

Issues in Crisis Intervention

The term "crisis" may be used to describe any intensely difficult period in an individual's lifetime. It may refer to physical, emotional, or various stressful circumstances which upset the person's normal style of coping with life. Slaikeu (1984) describes a crisis as "a temporary upset and disorganization, characterized chiefly by an individual's inability to cope with a particular situation using customary methods for problem solving ...." (p. 13).

Parad, Resnik, Ruben, Zusman, and Ruben (1975) describe crisis intervention as an active process aimed at lessening the impact of stress. For these authors there are two basic objectives associated with the process. The first is to decrease the effect of the stressor, and the second is to help those involved learn better ways of dealing with subsequent crises or problems. Thus, a crisis can be viewed as both a risk and an opportunity. It is an opportunity in the sense that individuals in crisis may learn more effective means of dealing with life's future problems.

Development of Crisis Intervention Theory

The concept of crisis intervention seems to have evolved over a number of decades. According to Lieb, Lipsitch, and Slaby (1973) much of the early work in dealing with crises was in the treatment of soldiers during combat experiences in an effort to prevent men from developing more serious disorders. Clinicians discovered that it was important to return soldiers to combat units with as little disruption in their routine as possible if they presented distress. Soldiers who realized they could avoid combat with psychiatric problems had an unfortunate tendency to regress and view themselves as disturbed.

A second major landmark in the development of crisis theory was the work of Lindemann (cited in Ewing, 1978). Lindemann followed 101 persons who experienced the death of a relative at a night club fire in Boston in 1942. He discovered that the individuals whom he studied had very similar reactions to the loss of their loved ones. He also described grief patterns and noted the possibility of helping individuals understand the stressful circumstances involved in the loss of a loved one.

Caplan (1964) is usually cited as having prepared the groundwork for crisis theory. He observed that crises are typically short lived and can be mastered through our usual means of coping. However, at times a person may be overwhelmed by a crisis situation, and usual methods of responding fail. He also found that during crises people are more open to help from others than during other times. According to Caplan there are four distinct phases associated with any crisis. The first is an initial phase in which the individual sees a problem and feels threatened. In this phase the individual uses his or her usual approaches to solving problems. The second phase occurs when the usual methods of coping fail and stress is further increased. The third phase occurs when continued attempts at solving the problem fail and new approaches are

attempted. If the problem is not resolved in the third phase, a
final stage of breakdown and more serious distress follows.

Parad et al. (1975) have also identified four stages of crisis
from a different perspective. These are (a) a precipitating event
or stressor, (b) perception of the event as a threat, (c) a state of
disequilibrium or crisis, and (d) resolution through the use of
effective coping measures. Crisis intervention would usually occur
during the third or disequilibrium stage.

There appear to be a variety of events that could qualify as
crises. These range from alcohol and drug abuse emergencies to
suicide and rape. Responses may be somewhat different, depending on
the type of crisis. Moreover, what may become a crisis could vary
among individuals and families.

Techniques of Intervention

Parad and Resnik (1975) have described the techniques involved
in crisis intervention as a sort of emotional and environmental
first aid. The most important skill which the intervener must have
is the ability to listen empathically in an effort to understand the
problems presented by the person in crisis. After the problem is
clarified, an attempt is made to stabilize and reassure the person.
Once this has occurred, an effort is made to find a more-or-less
immediate solution to the presenting problem. Often this involves
referral to an appropriate agency or involvement of relatives.
Parad and Resnik point out it is extremely important for the
intervention to be as immediate as possible.

Jacobson (cited in Aguilera & Messick, 1982) has pointed out

that crisis intervention may be either generic or individual. The
use of a generic approach assumes that a predictable pattern of
behavior is presented in most crises. This approach focuses on the
particular kind of crisis rather than the personality of an
individual. Any intervention is aimed at bringing about a
resolution to the crisis. Often these interventions may be carried
out by nonmental health professionals, since advanced training is
not necessarily required to understand a predictable situation or
maturational issue.

   The individual approach to crisis intervention is used when a
higher level of intervention is required. A careful assessment of
the person's mental state and history is usually involved. The
resulting treatment is primarily aimed at the particular needs of
the individual, but the emphasis is still placed on resolution of
the immediate crisis.

The Problem Solving Approach

   Aguilera and Messick (1982) discuss a problem solving approach
to crisis intervention. According to these authors, problem solving
follows a more or less predictable set of steps based on logical
reasoning. Some people may be more effective at finding problem
solutions than others. First, the problem must be correctly
assessed. This involves helping the individual clarify exactly what
is the crisis or problem. Next, the crisis intervener attempts to
find out what kinds of skills and resources the individual in crisis
may have. After that, it becomes possible to determine the person's

resources and some tentative solutions to the problem. Any actions are based on expectations of certain results from the process.

Crisis Intervention as Psychotherapy

Ewing (1978) has written a book titled Crisis Intervention as Psychotherapy. He describes crisis intervention as "a form of short-term psychotherapy...widely used in clinical settings" (p. 30). Ewing points out that crisis intervention focuses on the client's present problems but also seeks to develop more effective means for dealing with future problems and crises. In this type of intervention therapists must be more active and involved with clients than in many other forms of psychotherapy. While this approach prepares the client for further therapy, it is quite different from the traditional focus on personality issues.

Ewing discusses the applications of crisis intervention with children, families, and married couples. He notes that it sometimes is a useful alternative to traditional forms of marriage counseling which may take longer. He also points out that many recipients of crisis intervention return for follow-up therapy.

Specific Interventions

In the crisis intervention literature, there appears to be a growing number of examples of specific types of crisis interventions. Burgess and Baldwin (1981) have provided more than a dozen examples of specific kinds of crisis intervention. Several examples are discussed below.

Natural disasters. The National Institute of Mental Health (1978) has produced a volume and several training manuals which

describe crisis intervention programs for disaster victims. This
material outlines psychological needs in disasters and discusses
different impacts upon the mental health of the victims. Tierney
and Baisden (1979) have noted that various stresses on the community
mount as time passes following a disaster. While it appears that
disasters lead to extreme stress for victims, there is relatively
little known about long-term psychological symptoms. A great deal
more study needs to be done regarding how victims of disasters can
be helped through crisis intervention.

Suicide. An area related to crisis intervention which is of
great interest in this country is suicide prevention (e.g.,
Frederick, 1978). This is an extremely important problem because of
the profound effects on the survivors as well as the victims of
suicide (Hatton, Valente, & Rink, 1977). There is increasing
evidence that it is possible to predict suicide (Lettieri, 1974).
Crisis intervention with suicide appears to be an area of growing
specialization (Wekstein, 1979). Frederick (1983) has presented
specific techniques for dealing with the suicidal crisis, but a
discussion of these techniques is beyond the scope of this paper.

Rape crises. Rape has for some time been recognized as a
significant problem in this country (Brownmiller, 1976). In recent
years there has been a considerable amount written about helping
rape victims. Burgess and Baldwin (1981) discuss psychological
reactions to rape and provide guidelines for clinicians working with
rape victims. They emphasize that rape is a very complex issue, and
that recovery from rape can be difficult and lead to ongoing

stresses. Crisis intervention can help rape victims cope more
effectively and minimize the long-term negative side effects. In
many cities there exist specialized rape crisis centers.

Discussion

My study of crisis intervention uncovered a fairly large number
of books which deal with the topic. My impression is that it has
become a widely accepted approach in the mental health field.
Nevertheless, I failed to uncover much research which evaluates the
effectiveness of this approach. Ewing (1978) reviewed a few
relevant studies and concluded that there was, to date, no evidence
to support the effectiveness of crisis intervention. In fact, he
noted there have been only a few attempts to evaluate crisis
intervention.

This raises some interesting questions about the value of a
technique which relies only upon a brief intervention. Can we
really expect a form of help which just occurs when a person is in
crisis to lead to improvement in coping skills? While there seems
to be wide agreement that a crisis represents an opportune time for
intervention, I wonder if we might not discover that significant
changes in behavior require some longer interventions. Ewing has
noted that many recipients of crisis intervention return for
psychotherapy. It would be interesting to compare those who do and
those who do not in terms of future mental health problems.

Another interesting issue relates to who receives crisis
intervention and for what problems. One might hypothesize that
those who have the most potential to benefit were functioning

reasonably well prior to the crisis onset. Further, a delimited crisis would seem to suggest greater likelihood of improvement. Alternative arguments would suggest that poorer skills at onset allow more potential for development and that more substantial problems permit more opportunity for measurable change. My preference would be for the former hypotheses, but I found no relevant empirical evidence.

Summary

In this paper I have attempted to define crisis and outline various types of crisis intervention. Researchers in this area have discovered that crises follow more or less predictable patterns. Knowledge of these patterns can facilitate crisis intervention. Several approaches to crisis intervention were briefly discussed. There are a number of important issues related to the topic which require further study by clinicians and behavioral scientists. Nonetheless, it is accepted as an important avenue of intervention in the mental health field.

References

Aguilera, D. C., & Messick, J. M. (1982). Crisis intervention:
    Theory and methodology (3rd ed.). St. Louis: C. V. Mosby.

Brownmiller, S. (1976). Against our will: Men, women and rape.
    New York: Simon and Schuster.

Burgess, A. W., & Baldwin, E. A. (1981). Crisis intervention
    theory and practice: A clinical handbook. Englewood Cliffs,
    NJ: Prentice Hall.

Caplan, G. (1964). Principles of preventive psychiatry. New York:
    Basic Books.

Ewing, C. P. (1978). Crisis intervention as psychotherapy. New
    York: Oxford University Press.

Frederick, C. J. (1978). Current trends in suicidal behavior in
    the United States. American Journal of Psychotherapy, 32, 172–
    200.

Frederick, C. J. (1983). Suicide prevention procedures. In P. A.
    Keller & L. G. Ritt (Eds.), Innovations in clinical practice: A
    source book (Vol. 2, pp. 161–173). Sarasota, FL: Professional
    Resource Exchange.

Hatton, C. L., Valente, S. M., & Rink, A. (Eds.). (1977). Suicide:
    Assessment and intervention. New York: Appleton–Century–
    Crofts.

Lettieri, D. J. (1974). Suicidal death prediction scales. In A.
    T. Beck, H. L. P. Resnik, & D. J. Lettieri (Eds.), The
    prediction of suicide (pp. 163–192). Bowie, MD: The Charles
    Press Publishers.

Lieb, J., Lipsitch, I. I., & Slaby, A. E. (1973). The crisis team:
A handbook for the mental health professional. Hagerstown, MD:
Harper and Row.

National Institute of Mental Health. (1978). Training manual for
human service workers in major disasters (DHEW Publication No.
ADM 79-538). Washington, DC: U.S. Government Printing Office.

Parad, H. J., & Resnik, H. L. P. (1975). The practice of crisis
intervention in emergency care. In H. L. P. Resnik & H. L.
Ruben, (Eds.), Emergency psychiatric care: The management of
mental health crises (pp. 23-24). Bowie, MD: The Charles Press
Publishers.

Parad, H. J., Resnik, H. L. P., Ruben, H. L., Zusman, J., & Ruben,
D. D. (1975). Crisis intervention in emergency mental health
care: Concepts and principles. In H. L. P. Resnik, & H. L.
Ruben (Eds.), Emergency psychiatric care: The management of
mental health crises (pp. 1-21). Bowie, MD: The Charles Press
Publishers.

Slaikeu, K. A. (1984). Crisis intervention: A handbook for
practice and research. Boston: Allyn and Bacon.

Tierney, K. J., & Baisden, B. (1979). Crisis intervention programs
for disaster victims: A sourcebook and manual for smaller
communities (DHEW Publication No. ADM 79-675). Washington,
DC: U.S. Government Printing Office.

Wekstein, L. (1979). Handbook of suicidology. New York:
Brunner/Mazel.

APPENDIX B

SAMPLE RESEARCH
REPORT

The Effect of Classical Music

on the Growth of Tomato Plants[a]

Eva Green

Inane State University

Psy 403, Experimental Methods

February 30, 1984

---

[a]This is a fictitious report which is presented solely to
illustrate the recommended style for student research papers.
The experiment was never conducted and all results are simulated.

Abstract

There has been a growing interest in the effect of music on the development of plants. The present study tested the hypothesis that classical music would increase the growth of tomato plants. Twenty-five tomato plants were randomly assigned to either a classical music condition or a no music, control condition. In support of the hypothesis, the tomato plants exposed to classical music obtained greater height than the control group, both before the appearance of fruit and at maturity. Several variables were identified for further study.

The Effect of Classical Music

on the Growth of Tomato Plants

Psychologists, botanists, and certain musicians have had a

long-standing interest in the effects of music on the growth and

adjustment of plants (Tulip, 1982). One infrequently cited early

study (Freud & Bach, 1921) observed that plants in a professional

office where classical music was played for several hours each

evening grew stronger than a similar group of plants placed in

another room not exposed to the music. In spite of this

important early observation, surprisingly little research has

examined the effect of music upon plants (Inter-American

Foliatherapy Society, 1978).

Some years after the early Freud and Bach report, Watsen

(1942) discovered, quite by chance, that common garden weeds

fared poorly when exposed to popular music of the time played at

garden parties. Unfortunately, his findings were affected by a

number of confounding variables including beverage consumption by

party participants. Elles (cited in James, 1952) has also noted

that Watsen failed to control for the possible effects of

cognitive processes during his notorious parties. Hill and Dale

(1981) subsequently observed that the sensitive developmental

balance of growing plants is easily disrupted by certain

environmental factors, including noxious auditory stimuli.

More recently, Pansy (1965a, 1965b) measured the effects of

two variables, song and rain, upon the development of tomatoes.

While rainfall had a much greater influence on the growth of these plants, song proved to affect the color of tomatoes. A group of tomatoes exposed to light classical music took on a much deeper hue of red than a control group which was exposed to the recorded sounds of people eating at a party. The latter group never ripened.

The present study was designed to test the effects of classical music on the development of tomato plants. Based on the work of Pansy, it was hypothesized that tomatoes exposed to classical music would grow taller than plants not exposed to music.

Method

Subjects

The subjects were 24 Sunray tomato plants grown from seeds purchased from the Bright Wind Seed Company of Farmsworth, Iowa.

Apparatus

Plants were grown on two wooden tables in separate, sound isolated rooms of the Inane Psychology Laboratory. Three fluorescent growing lights were located 2 feet above a sterilized bed of potting soil on each of the growing tables. Two Anyo, continuous playing, stereo boom boxes (Model No. 5678) provided the sound stimuli. The speakers were played at a mean sound level of 65 decibels.

Procedure

The tomato seeds were randomly assigned to two groups of 12 plants: Classical Music (CM) and a No Music (NM) control. Seeds were planted according to instructions provided on the container.

The CM group was exposed to a continuous tape titled "Monti does Cleveland." The NM group was raised in a quiet room. Light from the fluorescent bulbs was continuous, plants were watered daily, and a steady air temperature of 25° C was maintained. At 35 days from planting, and prior to the appearance of fruit, an initial height measurement was taken. At 70 days from planting, all plants were sacrificed and a final height measurement was obtained.

Results

Mean heights for both groups obtained at the two observation points are shown in Table 1. As measured by t tests, the CM group was significantly taller than the NM group at both 35 days, t (22) = 3.21, p < .01, and 70 days, t (22) = 12.73, p < .001, after planting.

Insert Table 1 about here

Discussion

The results of this experiment support the hypothesis that classical music has an effect on the growth of tomato plants. Specifically, at observation points 35 and 70 days after planting, the tomato plants exposed to classical music were significantly taller than the no music control group.

The present study supports and improves on the earlier correlational works of Freud and Bach (1921), Watsen (1942), and Tulip (1982), by introducing experimental controls. However, the

experiment is relatively simple and does not address a number of
relevant issues such as changes in plant height over time or
plant weight.

While clearly illustrating that classical music can affect
plant development, many questions remain unanswered. For
example, it may be that the plants respond differentially to
various kinds of music. Further, this study does not touch on
the question of which type of music produces a better tomato
salad; data were not collected on the appearance of the fruit,
nor were taste tests formally included in the procedure.

In many ways, more questions were raised than answered by
this experiment. First, it seems important for future studies to
more clearly define the possible dependent variables for
examination, such as height, weight, and fruit quality. Next, it
seems important to consider the plants' developmental stages.
Certain sounds may be more growth enhancing or debilitating at
one stage than another. Finally, the addition of groups with
other types of sound would seem important.

References

Inter-American Foliatherapy Society. (1978). The subconscious

    life of plants (2nd ed.). Mexico City: Author.

Freud, S., & Bach, J. (1921). Classical music as a stimulus to

    growth in latency age greenery. Botanikos Erotika, 2, 8-13.

Hill, O., & Dale, T. (1981, July). Why garden parties aren't

    just for fun. Psychology Today, pp. 37-38, 42.

James, A. (1952). Plant enhancement through rational

    persuasion. Journal of Innovative Foliatherapy, 6, 167-173.

Pansy, I. M. (1965a). Plant physiology and behavior change. In

    A. Scales (Ed.), Psychophysiology. Philadelphia: Plenty

    Press.

Pansy, I. M. (1965b). Singing in the rain. American Journal of

    Psychological Gardening, 23, 129-135.

Tulip, R. (1982). A review of the effects of music upon the

    moral development of plants and insects. Journal of

    Ephemeral Psychology, 23, 117-128.

Watsen, J. W. (1942). Punish your weeds with music. In A.

    Johnson & W. Debardin (Eds.), Advances in foliatherapy

    through music (pp. 324-338). Cambridge: Ivy League Press.

Table 1

Mean Height in Centimeters for Classical Music and No Music

Groups at Two Observation Points

	Days from planting	
Group	35	70
Classical music	18.24	62.34
No music	15.78	45.98

INDEX

FEEDBACK QUESTIONNAIRE

We would appreciate your help in improving future versions of *How to Write Psychology Papers*. Please complete and return this brief questionnaire to the authors in care of the address at the bottom of this page. Thank you in advance for your feedback.

Are you: ☐An undergraduate student
☐A graduate student
☐A psychology instructor
☐Other type of user (please explain) _____

_____

For what purpose(s) did you use this guide? _____

_____

_____

_____

Overall, how helpful did you find it for your purposes?

:_____:_____:_____:_____:_____:_____:

Extremely Helpful   Not at all helpful

What did you like most about the guide? _____

_____

_____

_____

What did you like least about the guide? _____

_____

_____

_____

Other comments: _____

_____

_____

_____

Please return your comments to:
Peter A. Keller, Professional Resource Exchange, Inc./ P.O. Box 15560 / Sarasota, FL 34277-1560

NOTES

NOTES

NOTES

NOTES

905